THE COURAGEOUS ENTREPRENEUR

Cash Flow Strategies to Build Resiliency in Your Business

RINETTE LAGACE

First paperback edition: September 2019
Book cover design by: Toni Serofin
ISBN: 978-1-9991141-1-4

Published by: NB Communications
Diagrams and Puzzle Illustration © Rinette Lagace

This book is based on real events and people with whom I have worked. The names of people and their occupations have been changed to protect their identity.

Please note: the suggestions and solutions explained in this book are not applicable to every business or situation. It is important to seek professional advice to ensure that the best solutions are implemented for your specific company.

An entrepreneur is a brave soul with a desire to make a difference, armed with the knowledge and discernment to monetize their unique methods of providing a key product or service.

Table of Contents

INTRODUCTION

Approximately 3,580 businesses filed for bankruptcy in Canada in 2015.[1] This statistic does not even include the number of businesses who did not claim bankruptcy but were forced to close their doors. Does it make you think, "What conditions or issues occurred to force bankruptcy?"

The most serious part of these businesses declaring bankruptcy is the large amount of debt left behind—over $5 billion is owed to other businesses![2]

Every person who becomes an entrepreneur does so because they have a skill they can monetize. Of course, every entrepreneur believes that consumers cannot do without their product or service. The potential entrepreneur says, "Our business idea is a sure thing," or, "We'll make millions!" Now, that hopeful entrepreneur is in the trenches of running their business; issues keep creeping up, creating bigger and bigger problems. They want to know where things went wrong or how to get back on track. Is this you?

In North America, 98.2% of businesses are considered small businesses. In Canada, small businesses employed almost 69.7% of private sector workers in 2012—that's 7.7 million people across the country![3] By being an entrepreneur, YOU are a key driving force in our economy!

---

[1] Insolvency Statistics in Canada-December 2018, Office of the Superintendent of Bankruptcy. http://www.ic.gc.ca/eic/site/bsf-osb.nsf/eng/br04038.html

[2] How Small Business Vs. Personal Bankruptcy Are Different in Canada, Susan Ward. https://www.thebalancesmb.com/how-do-personal-bankruptcy-and-business-bankruptcy-differ-2947903

[3] 10 Things you Didn't Know About Canadian Smes. https://www.bdc.ca/en/articles-tools/business-strategy-planning/manage-business/pages/10-things-didnt-know-canadian-sme.aspx?intlnk=rightbox

What is considered a small business? A small business is defined by the number of employees. Any business that employs 1-99 people, including the owner or proprietor, is considered a small business. Of these small businesses, 55% are made up of only 1-4 people.

I truly believe in my definition of an entrepreneur: A brave soul with a desire to make a difference, partnered with the knowledge and discernment to monetize their unique methods of providing a key product or service.

Courage is necessary in entrepreneurship: you are often betting all of your savings, time from your family and sometimes your well-being is on the line. Over the years, I have found that the key traits to successful business ownership is discernment, by this I mean you must have the ability to distinguish the value in each decision you make. Especially when the consequences are keenly beneficial or detrimental to your organization. It is key that an entrepreneur is both open to acknowledging their faults and strong enough to resolve or find ways to effectively address their weaknesses.

Successful business owners are good at what they do and that is why they can earn money from their skills. Part of their success is the ability to quickly recover from mistakes and implement new strategies when things go awry.

So why are so few business owners equipped for success? A new business is often overwhelming. There are several reasons why a business can succeed while an almost identical business fails. My goal with this book is to arm you with keys to avoiding the common pitfalls that many companies face. A business owner's skill is making money with their craft, sales, or services, yet they might be lacking in managing the day-to-day business details. A business owner might not understand how to handle everyday tasks well, whether it results in mismanagement, overpaying for basic expenses, encountering unexpected expenses, or handling unforeseen changes in the economy. Over time, these deficiencies can put a small business in danger of failure.

Consider this book as a guide to help you anticipate and navigate these threats. This book is a collection of stories through which I share my 25-year experience as a bookkeeper for various businesses. My hope is to shed light on the importance of skillfully handling the day-to-day aspects of running of your business so you can have what we all desire, a profit.

My experience encompasses businesses of all sizes, from individual proprietors to property management companies, non-profits, corporations and regional districts. Although business structures may vary, there are many common threads: all businesses have key areas that owners tend to overlook where they can save thousands of dollars and avoid a struggle in managing their cash flow.

As you read this book, be open to possibilities and be willing to implement simple changes to increase your success as a business owner. There are always circumstances out of your control that may affect your business; by preparing yourself, you can mitigate the potential damage that a lack of cash flow can cause. There are no guarantees when you start a business, the bottom-line is that your daily choices will make or break your company.

1. THE CASH-FLOW PROBLEM

"Entrepreneurs believe that profit is what matters most in a new enterprise. But profit is secondary. Cash flow matters most."
~ *Peter Drucker*

Peter Drucker writes that entrepreneurs believe profit is what matters most in a new enterprise. But profit is secondary. Cash flow matters most.[4] Hands down, managing cash flow is the biggest challenge for business owners. The definition of "cash flow" is the processes of money coming in and going out of your business. The goal is to have more cash flowing in than going out, also known as profit. Another way to look at it is, "cash today, gone tomorrow and repeat."

Most businesses view the amount of cash coming in as a key measurement of a successful business, but it is the day-to-day expen-ses incurred that keeps the lights on, brings in the products, pays the staff (your main asset), bills, and the suppliers/vendors you need to serve your clients or customers. In the early stages of a business, profit certainly is important but it is only one part of a successful business gauge. How is your cash flow or available liquidity within your business? Liquidity is the term for available cash on hand that you use to pay for the expenses mentioned. Have you heard the term "cash is king"? This is still very much today's reality.

Awareness of Your Cash Flow Situation

Over the years, I have had the opportunity to work with and for some brilliant business owners. Some were funny, some outright

---

[4] 12 Thought-provoking Cash Flow Quotes and Expressions. https://www.paypie.com/blog/2018/09/12-thought-provoking-cash-flow-quotes-and-expressions/

outrageous, and some, despite their intellectual brilliance, encountered errors which took their once-thriving businesses to the brink of existence, effectively forcing the closure of their businesses or the need to claim bankruptcy. At the very least, their lack of focus on cash flow costed them thousands of dollars in extra charges, fees, and lost income. In turn, those choices detrimentally affected the available funds for servicing day-to-day operations which also affected the sustainability or success of their businesses.

It is not how smart you are, it is all about awareness— awareness of snags, potential setbacks, compliance issues or unexpected situations that start demanding your attention. Knowing how cash moves in and out of your business is crucial. Often, the regular daily issues that require an owner's attention can take you away from staying on top of cash flow details. Slowly and unsuspectingly, this inattention can syphon the cash from your company.

Cash flow problems always come with warning signs, you just need to know what these warning signs look like. When you do know, you and your managers have a chance to address the issues. Subtle warning signs are easily overlooked and ultimately, the
cumulative effect of ignoring these warning signs results in a significant lack of available cash flow to the business.

We are going to use Johnny's story throughout this book. Johnny, a mechanic, strolled into my office one morning. With an excited look, he proceeded to tell me his plans for purchasing a brand new mechanic truck to offer a new service his clients. He asked me—his bookkeeper— "We can afford to do this, right?"

I hesitated to give a flat out "yes" or "no" as there is rarely a simple answer. The idea was a great one with a lot of potential, however, I knew his business was tight on cash flow. As my sister, a Certified General Accountant (CGA) explains, "In business and taxes, a simple question rarely has a simple answer. There are always a number of factors that will dictate your answer and a number of variables which may affect which option or answer would be more correct for each scenario."

Even a simple question such as, "Can I pay out a flat mileage rate per kilometre for the use of my personal vehicle?" Well, that depends on the business structure: are you a proprietor or are you incorporated? As a proprietor, the answer is "no"; as an incorporated business, yes you can. Then there are specific rules around how much is an acceptable amount to pay per kilometre without it becoming a taxable expense.

You are probably wondering what my answer was to Johnny's initial question, whether or not he could afford a new mechanic truck. The process we used to decide what realistic options were available to his business will be touched on throughout this book. Johnny's real issue, hands down, was managing cash flow in his business, which is often the biggest challenge for all business owners.

There is no magic equation and no easy outs, it is all about diligence in your management skills, in your expectations of your staff or bookkeeper and in paying attention to the small details that are often right in front of you.

This book is divided into three main sections: Making Money, Saving Money, and the tools for forming new strategies, which includes the process of Evaluation and Review for adapting or evolving your business.

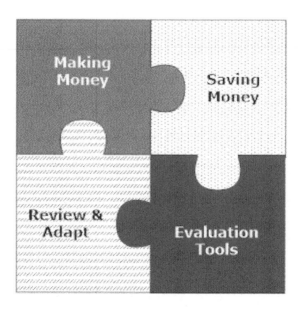

Many people are unaware of the many rules, expectations, and filing requirements (compliance issues) required by the Canadian government (and in principle, apply in other countries as well). Although your main skill set is what makes you money, if you do not understand the key requirements of a business owner and how the game of business works in our environment, it will limit your level of success.

Over the years, I have encountered many "what the heck" moments in working with business owners, managers, accounting firms and auditors. By sharing some of these stories in this book, explaining why things have occurred and providing the tools to implement protective processes, I hope to help you, as a business owner, improve your chance of business success.

After reading this book, you will be able to identify the warning bells in daily business practices that require your attention. You will be equipped with the tools necessary to avoid the negative consequences that would occur if these went ignored.

1.1 Common Threats to Your Cash Flow

*The difference between profit and cash flow is that a lack
of cash flow is what can and will sink a business.*

How realistic are business owners in predicting revenue or sales? Although there are always outside factors out of your control, you should always consider a realistic value with some room for error. Unfortunately, most business owners **overestimate their income, and, at the same time, underestimate potential expenses**. They also fail to anticipate a cash shortage and run out of the money needed to keep business running. One example of a cash shortage is a business' slow or off-season, which, if not adequately planned for, can have very negative effects on a business.

How can businesses avoid this? The answer may not lie in the numbers themselves, but in the benefit of evaluating all the potential risk factors and analyzing the information derived.

Consider Your Everyday Costs

A common error is putting everything you have into the start-up phase, leaving yourself short on day-to-day operating funds or working capital. As a result, you may find yourself in personal debt in order to cover expenses. This debt often lingers for years after the business closes.

Many business owners feel strongly about their service or product and will heavily invest at the outset, believing they will make lots of money in the first year. Although the potential may exist, they leave themselves short for the main phase of business— the building and operating phase. This is where investment into staffing, advertising, supplies and rent must be allocated. It is wise to have a buffer in place to cover these regular costs.

Another common error is tying up money in a large accounts receivables balance. This means that your money is tied up in customers still owing you for your products and services. Although it is money coming and owed to the business, don't rely on these to pay for your day-to-day expenses.

Below are a few examples of common practices that can potentially create a lack of cash flow:

- Lower than anticipated profits or sales.
- Investing in too much stock or inventory.
- Allowing customers too much credit.
- Unplanned expenses (this is a big one).
- Paying for exorbitant expenses that may not be legitimate.
- Seasonal business rhythm with long down times.
- Expanding or growing too quickly.
- Not following up on dishonoured cheques or payments.
- Late payment fees or excessive bank charges due to shortage of funds, or funds not coming in on a regular basis.
- Late fees, fines, non-filing charges, and interest on government remittances.
- Excessive credit card interest charges.
- Declining gross profit margins due to increase in product costs, increasing freight and or fuel costs to receive the products.
- Ongoing losses accumulating each year.
- Spending too much upfront.
- Living large way too quickly.
- Purchasing items that are not necessary at certain points in your business.
- Poor management skills and/or people management skills.
- Theft by staff.
- Fraud.

- Lack of established systems and protocols.
- Operating an open till (where the owner just takes out whatever and whenever they want, with no accounting of these transactions).
- Lack of policies and/or verification processes.

Every business owner wants to avoid having cash sucked out from under them. It is important to remain aware of warning signs and be prepared to take action!

Below is a diagram showing the benefits of available cash-on-hand, and conversely, the detrimental effects due to the inability to access cash when needs arise.

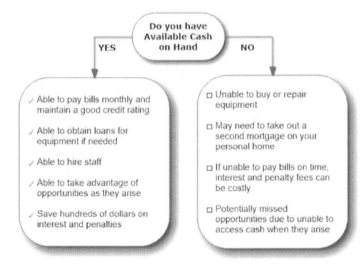

Clarify the differences between "profit" and "cash flow" as this will help you make the best decisions for your business.

In Johnny's case, his business was certainly making a profit. Perhaps adding another service to his business would indeed provide more value to his clients. The key for Johnny is, could he maintain the added costs of leasing or purchasing this new mechanic truck, outfit it with all the necessary tools and ensure he had a qualified person to run the truck and service their clients?

Just because Johnny was running his company at a profit, does this mean he has the available cash to maintain loan payments?

Profit = Making Money

Profit is the difference between the total income generated, minus all the expenses paid. Your income statement is your gauge on how well you are doing and if your company is in a profitable position.

Cash flow = Managing Money

Cash flow is the difference between the cash going in and going out of your business. Income is not counted until received and expenses are not calculated until payments are made. A company's balance sheet is where cash flow is gauged. This shows if you have enough money to pay the bills or if your money is tied up in accounts receivables. Accounts receivables may end up being a waiting game. There is no guarantee they will get paid in the time needed for you to pay your own bills on time.

The difference between profit and cash flow is that a lack of cash flow is what sinks a business. Remember, just because a business is making a profit does not mean it has enough cash flow to sustain itself.

1.2 Growing Too Fast

Expansion has many moving parts, although it can be exciting, there are a lot of unknown variables.

You need to proceed prudently. Most people will ask me, "How is expanding my business a problem?" Here is an example of the issues that can occur in any expansion:

Growing Beyond Control

There is this one small company that developed a powdered product I'll call the "wonder mix". This powder "wonder mix" provided health benefits that everyone was looking for in today's market of proactive health improvement. Initially, this company started out as relatively small, attending local farmer's markets and fairs to get exposure for their product. They employed two, part-time staff and the owners only wanted a part-time gig as they were technically in retirement. However, after a while, they were interested in expanding their sales, which in turn, would increase their income levels during this time. So, they went on *Dragon's Den*, a Canadian television show where entrepreneurs pitch successful businesspeople for potential investment from them. The exposure they received from that one televised show increased their sales beyond expectations.

The "wonder mix" owners were excited to see their little part-time business become a sensation from one, 15-minute episode. Yet, the exposure quickly resulted in demand that exceeded their ability in the following days and weeks.

The owners suddenly had to look at ways to meet their instant notoriety and increased demands! Orders were piling up and sales went through the roof. So, they did what every business owner does, they hired more staff, ordered more packaging materials, and tried to stay on top of their orders. However, their current operational model was still not conducive to their growth.

Normally, a business owner would wish for success like this, however, what ensued was unhappy customers cancelling their orders and funds returned. Until the company could update their operations, they had to limit the orders they could actually fill.

The costs of operations increased, the owners had to secure financing and were both working full-time. An increase in staff issues occurred because appropriate systems were not in place, human resource policies and procedures were not developed because there was a lack of skilled management in that area.

This was no longer a fun, part-time gig for the owners. Their huge growing pains and resulting issues were overwhelming!

This little company faced further change when they finally did adapt to new systems. Everything changed: they adopted an updated ordering system that could handle large orders, they purchased, implemented, and maintained new systems and machinery, and there were changes in staff and associated management and policies. Then there was the constant tweaking of those systems and operations.

Yes, this company did indeed become successful, but it was a painful experience for the owners and their staff. Needless to say, this went from a part-time gig to a more-than- full-time undertaking just to manage the day-to-day needs and the many decisions required.

To have a happier staff, the owners spent lots of money on a trip for their staff and families. When the owners realized the costs involved in such an endeavour, they were unable to repeat this perk. Only after reviewing the first year of growth did they realize they were overspending, their plans were all over the place, they had a huge tax bill and were beginning their second year of growth behind the eight-ball. Growth certainly had its challenges.

Their ideal growth would have included implementing new systems in phases—expanded upon at a later time. This takes planning. Not only is smooth growth dependent upon how prepared you are to add, adapt, change, increase and train staff, but you also need cash flow to accomplish these goals. You need access to financial resources or potential investors. Each new system implemented takes time and resources.

Below is a list of some potential warning signs that indicate you may be growing too fast. Can you relate to any of these points?

- You are still collecting payments from accounts receivables from over a year prior. Having your cash flow tied up with accounts receivables—especially anything over 90 days—is a concern and will likely turn into bad debt.

- You are paying loans or bills still owed from when the business was small. This could mean that you have either overspent in the beginning stages of your business; your profits are very low or in the negatives.

- Still waiting to collect from unpaid receivables or invoices. These are invoices for products or services in which you have already paid out to cover all the expenses in providing the service or product such as paying for staff, paying to have the products the customer now has, yet no payment from the customer has been received.

- Does your staff have the knowledge and ability to do the work as you expand?

You may have heard of the *Peter Principle* in which employees are promoted based on the success shown in their current position until they reach their "level of incompetence".[5] Many entrepreneurs are often looking for someone to fill a void until they have the funds to hire a more qualified, specifically-trained person. The *Peter Principle* can work if the employee is ambitious and wants the challenge, but as a manager of your business, you need to proceed with caution—you would not want to set up someone for failure because they lack knowledge or training.

Giving Away the Farm

If you are using personal finances or your credit to get more loans for financing your offerings, you are essentially paying to carry your client. Sounds backwards doesn't it? If you have to pay for the labour, the products and supplies to provide a service for which you have not been paid, this is a big problem. How long can a business offer free products and services before going broke?

No company can afford this in the long term. The reason you are in business is to generate income, a cash flow for you to grow your business and feed your family.

I have a very creative client, Sara, who works hard at bringing her ideas to fruition. In order to show professionalism and highlight the quality of her workshops, Sara would spare no expense. Her workshops location was in a beautiful, ritzy hotel. She had colourful brochures, paid for staff to set up and organize, paid for snacks, coffee and an event host. The comfort of her participants was paramount. However, there are a number of ways to accomplish the same goals without such a high expense. To top it off, not only was she the one helping to check people in and take care of issues, she was also the keynote speaker and had to organize other speakers! I am feeling exhausted just describing all the tasks she took on.

---

5 The Peter Principle: Why Things Always Go Wrong, by Dr. Laurence J Peter, Raymond Hull

The workshops were no small feat and she bore the entire expense for the event herself. Yes, each participant would pay a fee, however, Sara ended up on the hook for expenses that the participant fees were unable to cover. Each year, she was getting a new business loan to cover the unpaid expenses from the year prior and have a little set aside to help tackle new expenses planned for the current year's events. Not only was Sara not drawing a wage from the business, the word "lucrative" is not a word I would use to describe her business.

Sara wanted her events to operate like the large companies with which she was in competition, but by doing so, she put herself into deeper and deeper debt each year. Here are some steps Sara should have considered:

1. **Determining her breakeven point.** Establishing this after reviewing overall costs and potential revenue is crucial in deciding whether or not it's even worth moving forward with the event. Calculating how many participants are needed to cover the costs is a good gauge for a breakeven point.

2. **Overestimating expenses and underestimating revenues.** This would provide a more realistic margin of error in which to operate. She would be better informed in selecting room size for the event and choosing the services included in the event. For example, instead of providing a rich meal, perhaps offering soup and sandwiches or lunch might be a more affordable option.

3. **Sharing the event costs.** Partnering with other companies who are in-line with the purpose of the event instead of Sara bearing the entire cost of the event herself could save her from carrying so much debt. Cost could be proportionate to each party involved or sponsorship packages arranged.

4. **Tailoring the marketing plan.** Perhaps Sara's marketing plan is flawed or too broad. Arranging a brainstorm with or polling staff, potential partners or potential customers will help target the right market and inform how to market to them effectively. Clearly identifying the target market—even creating a profile of the ideal client—is helpful in knowing how to attract them. For example, young people are social media savvy so digital marketing is their language. If the target is seniors, they still like reading papers and perhaps listen to the radio. Perhaps there are groups she should join or speak at to learn more about the target audience's lifestyle and expectations.

There are so many options in marketing. Sara would benefit in the long run from an openness to suggestions and change.

Acting bigger than you can operate within will always be detrimental to your company.

1.3 The Optics of Your Business

"Prove yourself to yourself, not others." – My Mother

It is exciting to see your company making money! Things are going along well and there is lots of potential. Perhaps you feel you can now show your clients that you are a successful businessperson and have to look the part. So, you buy a new car, get the best clothes, put your kids into nice schools and go on extravagant holidays.

Whoa! I wish people would really think on this. Stop here and really think about what a successful businessperson in your industry looks like to you. How is their business structured? What does it look like? What type of vehicle do they drive? Are they always on vacation? If they do take long vacations and drive a fancy car, did they purchase these in the first few years of business?

Take the time to clearly identify what you believe a successful person in your business would do, would look like and value in their lifestyle. Mentally make this list now but do take some time to write out what you believe are the traits of a successful businessperson. Consider the questions below:

- Are you picking up the tab for expensive lunch meetings with clients?
- Are you taking extra vacation time and spending a lot of time away?
- Do you purchase top-of-the-line items you previously thought you could not afford?
- Do you feel like you NEED to have a fancy new car, even though your other one was perfectly fine?
- Are you habitually buying rounds for your friends?

- Are your friends now requesting to borrow money from you?
- Are you ignoring what your bank account is saying based on the knowledge that you have a lot of accounts receivables?
- Are you concerned about looking a certain way or having certain things to prove that you are indeed a successful businessperson?
- Do you wish to be noticed, respected or want people to look up to you?
- Do you want to be special?

Many of the values indicated in the above questions are not necessarily negative, but it may not be the right time to act upon them if your business' cash flow isn't adequate.

Think about the oil boom. Many young guys head off to the Alberta oil fields with the promise of making the big bucks, and they do! However, have you noticed how many spend it like its burning holes in their pockets? They get a mortgage to match their income level, the new big truck, the ATV, the snowmobile and other toys. If they have a family to support, they buy new "toys" or undergo expensive renovations on their homes. I, myself, have a son that did well in the oil fields yet has nothing to show for it other than debt, or at least a vehicle with debt.

What if the oil market crashes and these men don't have their oil field jobs anymore? They may be left without jobs or have to take on jobs which pay a fraction of their previous incomes. They are left with a mountain of debt which they can no longer manage.

I have known many business owners that found themselves in similar predicaments due to overspending or experiencing difficult times such as a recession, yet they all still have a family to feed.

One of my clients ran their business on the edge of bankruptcy for years and we had to juggle which bills could be paid this week and which could be paid the next week so they could make payroll. In this case, my clients had the rare experience—and some luck—in eventually selling their business, allowing them to finally get out of debt and have a base to start up again in a different circumstance. I certainly do not recommend anyone waiting and hoping for this to happen; it is rare and not always the right thing to do.

In both scenarios, the error commonly made is living large without the ability to maintain that "large life". Sadly, this is a far more common scenario than we think. Even I have succumbed to this. Did I have to buy the fastest computer to do my job? Didn't the older computer still work? Was that Black Friday buy really a good investment? Did I buy it because it was on sale, therefore justifying the cost, or did it really have everything I needed? Could I have waited? Staying within your means and even below your means is key. As my mother says, "You have nothing to prove to anyone but yourself."

What Success Looks Like

What does success mean to you and what does it look like?

The clients I see as truly successful show it by how they treat their staff, customers, suppliers and families, all in balance with their cash flow. These are usually more important priorities than expensive clothes or flashy cars.

1.4 The Mind-Set of a Business Owner

"Independent business owners are heroes, by my definition, because they are really putting it on the line, working very hard, risking it all, and in some cases, taking home less than some of their employees. They create not only jobs, but also a really amazing experience." – Dan Price

The entrepreneurial person has a mindset that is unique from an employee's. The difference is in the way an entrepreneur approaches challenges and/or mistakes. Entrepreneurs have the drive to constantly improve or try a different approach when one approach fails. Entrepreneurs are persistent. This commitment is a trait that many entrepreneurs rely upon in order to succeed. Not everyone is able to be an entrepreneur, and some will definitely be happier to remain as an employee.

Entrepreneurial Mindset	Employee Mindset
Paid by results.	Paid by time regardless of the results.
Thrives upon risk	Averse to risk
Okay with lack of balance as they know it can be a 24/7 lifestyle	Thrives on a work / life balance
Always looking for ways to improve upon their weaknesses or will draw upon their strengths	Usually do not want to admit they have weaknesses as it is viewed as a negative quality
Are happy to delegate tasks	Will do it themselves
They would be bored working as an employee	The income potential is limited to the amount of time they are available to work
Hire those smarter than themselves	People smarter than themselves are viewed as a threat

Over the years, I have watched many business owners' personalities change when they take on their ownership roles. In my experience, it is a necessary change, with many positive aspects.

I have heard comments like, "He is so stuck up since his business took off," or "She asks way too many questions." These people are the same people, but they are now required to look at things differently. Often, others may take these changes personally rather than step back and ask why.

A shift in a business owner's mindset is usually due to various factors which include one or a combination of the following scenarios:

The realization that you will be living without a stable, predictable income. This is probably one of the hardest things to plan around, especially if your previous situation was no employment at all or if your family depends upon you as the sole income earner.

Knowing that, as an entrepreneur, you no longer have "set hours," but long days and low pay (if any) in the early years.

A huge, scary tax bill for which was not planned for. The government can and will be very demanding of a business owner's attention to their taxes. It is far too common that when business owners start out, they do not always think to set aside money for taxes, spending it before the tax bill arrives.

Being the sole decision-maker. A business owner might make over 100 key decisions each and every day. It's daunting and stressful finding solutions to issues for which you did not anticipate. Especially when your decisions affect others such as their families, their staff, their customers or clients. It can be hard to stay positive and see the good in a situation which does not seem so positive on the surface.

Requests for community involvement and donations. Once you are in business, many groups from varying ages and sources may start coming to you regularly for a donation to their cause, a free gift for their fundraiser or sponsorship involvement! As an entrepreneur, community groups will often solicit you for some type of support. Of course, you want to give back to your community as it is great advertising! However, how much can you give before it negatively affects your business? Do you have a plan on how to address this? Although donations are an important part of building a business in a community, without clear guidelines, it can become a drain.

As a business owner, ask these questions to determine if a cause is one to which you would like to contribute:

- Are they a reputable group?
- Are they well known in the community?
- Have they been around for a while?
- Is this a cause that is important to you and your family?
- How often do they need financial support?
- What is their cycle of donation campaigning and am I comfortable with it? Do I want to give seasonally, annually, etc.?

Be Aware of Scams

As an entrepreneur, it is often important to your success to give back to the community that serves you. However, do your due diligence. There are many scams out there and even the most knowledgeable of business owners has fallen prey. In today's business climate, businesses face relentless scams and fraudulent practices every day. Your emails are full of them and it only takes one unsuspecting person to make an honest mistake which can cost you thousands. Worst case scenario, a scam can force a business to close.

One of the more common scams involves the real estate market. On the day of closing a rather large real estate deal, a seemingly legitimate request comes in stating there is a change in wire instructions. These changes require the buyer transfer money to a fraudster and not to the intended recipient! Hundreds and thousands of dollars have been sent to the wrong person, abruptly ending a sale and the buyer losing thousands of dollars. This is one example of why business owners change the way they think, talk, and operate day-to-day. They want to ensure they do not fall victim to such situations.

If you would like to know more about scams and some tips to protect yourself, you'll find more information in Chapter 3.12. There is also a list of websites in the Appendix.

Employees are an Asset

As your company grows, there comes a need for more staff. This is often looked at two very different ways. One is viewing staff as another challenge or babysitting job. Understandable, as people have very different needs and challenges which affect our well-being and our abilities as employees. The second is to treat them as your greatest asset!

Your employees are your biggest advertising campaign. They tell others if they are happy or unhappy at work, if they love what you stand for and what you do in the community. The key is to treat your staff as you would wish to be treated. There are many ways business owners like to engage, inspire and encourage staff to be the best they can. Dan Price is a great example of this.

Writer Gaby Hinslif tells Price's story in the *Huffington Post* in 2018.[6] Price, CEO of Gravity, introduced a minimum salary of

$70,000 for his employees as this was considered the base living wage for the area. Now, this CEO admittedly made a "crazy amount of money" so he slashed his own wage of over a million dollars a year to make this happen.

You could imagine the initial fallout from his co-owner (his own brother), and the Board of Directors. This was not a popular move. However, since Price moved forward with his brave move, Gravity has seen an increase of 80% in clientele! Price did not define business success solely on financial results, but also on how the pay raises would change the lives of his staff and the resulting optics.

Although this would not be a likely scenario for smaller businesses with limited resources and staffing needs, the point of this story is that our employees have the same wants, needs, and desires as we do. Having a wage that enables your staff to live life without too much struggle provides a lot of value.

When Price was interviewed in 2015 after raising the base wage, he said, "Independent business owners are heroes, by my definition, because they are really putting it on the line, working very hard, risking it all, and in some cases, taking home less than some of their employees. They create not only jobs, but also a really amazing experience."[7]

Looking back at the changes implemented in his company, Price stated that the return was better than anything he could have imagined. He saw his staff saving three times the amount from prior, he saw far more staff becoming first-time homeowners

---

[6] This CEO Took A Pay Cut To Give Employees $70,000 A Year. Now He's Battling Amazon., Gaby Hinsliff. https://www.huffpost.com/entry/dan-price-minimum-wage_n_5afd3d8ee4b06a3fb50dcf28

[7] Gravity Payment's Dan Price on How he Measures Success After His $70k Experiment – Jim Ludema & Amber Johnson. https://www.forbes.com/sites/amberjohnson-jimludema/2018/08/28/gravity-payments-dan-price-on-how-he-measures-success-after-his-70k-experiment/#68e2728e174b

THE COURAGEOUS ENTREPRENEUR · 27

and having families. Prior to 2015, only a few became homeowners and savings were almost nonexistent. This was the impact that he used to measure his company's success: he saw people able to improve their lives. For Price, people came first.

Think about a person or manager for whom you have worked that you admire. What were some of their admirable traits? Perhaps you admire how they handled a situation, a difficult person or a complaint. How did this person make a difference for you? Did you work together to solve a problem? Were they open to suggestions or alternative options in accomplishing a task if key elements were met?

Management Strategies

Being deliberate and methodical is the key to success in any business. Being reactionary and stressed only creates blocks in solving problems internally and for your customers. Choose one thing to address at a time, focus on learning that task, then address the others as you can.

As a business owner, you may be interested in terminology used to describe some of the tremendously successful business owners of our day—Bill Gates, Steve Jobs, Reed Hastings, Elon Musk and others. They are described as having a trait called "integrative complexity".[8] This trait is defined as the ability to interpret and integrate multiple perspectives and possibilities, enabling the person to come up with a variety of contingencies. A common trait among these business owners is the ability to see both the big picture all the way down to the smallest details.

The ability to evaluate a situation with discernment is the real change that occurs when a person becomes an entrepreneur. The

[8] Studies Show That People Who Have High "integrative Complexity" Are More Likely To Be Successful, Michael Simmons. https://medium.com/accelerated-intelligence/studies-show-that-people-who-have-high-integrative-complexity-are-more-likely-to-be-successful-443480e8930c

hard times and lessons that a person learns through their business will greatly inform how they choose to run their business overall. A wise entrepreneur resolves to continue moving forward with their new-found knowledge, all the while knowing that with each stumble, they are getting better, smarter and more discerning with their business. This approach ultimately increases their chances of reaching their goals.

Reading books on building a resilient, positive mind-set are available all over the marketplace. These types of books are often best sellers but this book is not one of those books. I only recognize the value that these bring for business owners as it helps provide another point of view, an opinion, or at the very least, another way of looking at the same situation so that an entrepreneur can see an opportunity instead of an obstacle.

1.5 Building Your Empire

As an entrepreneur, we are all building our own empires.
It is just a matter of scale.

All businesses have what I and many others call a "PITB factor", or "pain in the butt" factor. You may have heard of this term before and it is an important (and unavoidable) part of business. Different businesses have differing level of challenges (PITB factors) and each stage requires different supports. Most times, people want to use these differing business levels as stepping stones. One example of a PITB factor is the complications that may arise when a business grows too fast. Handled improperly or without the right supports, this PITB factor can self-destruct your business.

SEBO: Handling It All

Frank is a self-employed business owner (SEBO). A plumber, Frank, is extremely picky about his work, as he should be. He is very busy, sought out for his skill, knowledge and attention to detail. Because he is in such demand, he is able to charge a premium for his time. As a result, he is very successful at self-employment. However, he has two weaknesses: one, he is not patient enough to take on an apprentice and teach them to his high standards; two, his skill with paperwork does not match his trade skills. He is talented and doing very well for himself but is always behind on his paperwork.

Now there are two very common issues here for SEBOs. Firstly, Frank's business is limited to his available billable hours only; income solely rests upon his availability. The ability to generate the income to feed his family and support the day-to-day bills is on his shoulders alone. This effectively limits the business' income potential. If he is sick, injured, or he wants to take his family on vacation, the work stops.

Secondly, since keeping track of the paperwork is not his strength, he relies on his spouse to help keep him organized, ensure his billing is sent out, regular remittances are filed, and all is done in a timely fashion. These processes are paramount to his success but because of his lack of skill in administrative tasks, there is sometimes stress around this aspect of his business.

Pros for this type of business: It requires a minimal amount of start-up and it has a relatively low PITB factor.

Cons for this type of business: The cons with this type of business include limited income potential and the inability to carry on should the owner be unable to work. No work equals no income.

BAB: Getting Staff to Do the Work

Now, I have another client, Thomas, who specializes in the transportation business. He relies on a full complement of staff— other fellow transportation experts that are able to do the same work as he. Thomas would be happy to say he "knew nothing" and trusted his staff to "keep the business going". This is a big step for a business owner. This type of business owner relies heavily on the ability to lead or direct a group of people. Thomas identified and relies upon each of his employee's strengths to build his business. He understands he does not have to do everything himself to build success or achieve a low PITB factor.

What many business owners miss is that, "blind trust" is not the most intelligent strategy for owning a business. Overall, a better outcome is achieved by implementing the "trust and confirm!"[9] model.

In Thomas' business, he contracted two part-time bookkeepers to ensure all the invoices went out and the bills and government remittances were paid on time. He also relied on his accountant to verify the data annually. This freed up Thomas to focus on making money for the business.

Thomas also had one key person managing the staff—the transportation experts—including he himself. Thomas is fully aware of his shortcomings as a manager, so he entrusts someone else to manage the day-to-day operations of his business. When consulted, he provides his "ok" based upon previously-established company policies and expectations. Then he trusts his staff to do their jobs. This is not to say he would not step in and deal with situations like a necessary firing, but these tasks are few and far between because he also makes a point of letting his staff know they are valued. In this scenario, Thomas built his business slowly, starting out as a SEBO (with his wife doing the books) and expanding into a "building a business" type of owner, or "BAB".

You are, for the most part, hands off, and must hire staff to carry out the work. You are the salesperson or the face of your company. You are great at generating business and rely on persons with basic skills to fulfill those needs. You have business savvy and can build something in which others can be a part. You give the day-to-day responsibilities to staff while you drum up the work.

Pros for this type of business: As exampled by Thomas, the pros of a BAB business include: making money even when the owner is away or unable to work, the income generated increases as do his expenses, an increased need to stay on top of day-to-day cash flow and the accounts receivables.

---

[9] 2003-2019 ZD -CMS Driven – leadergrow.com. Bob Whipple.
https://www.leadergrow.com/articles/443-trust-but-verify

In this case, an owner is working *on* their business, not *in* their business. This model can have a medium PITB factor because you have managers and staff that deal with day-to-day tasks. You may have heard that building an empire needs a visionary. That visionary handles the high-level aspects of their business while staff provide the services. As an entrepreneur, you are building our own empire. It is just a matter of scale.

Cons for this type of business: Some of the cons of a BAB: a large outlay of start-up funds are required, payroll issues, staffing, policies and procedures are required, and a full complement of team members with different strengths are needed to keep the business running smoothly.

The PITB factor with a BAB is quite high. This can be due to human resource realities such as hiring, firing and day-to-day staff issues. Some of the cons of being the funder for this type of company are: you are reliant on your staff to provide the services, there is always an attrition rate for changes in personnel, or staff may perform at varying levels of competency. Also, as the owner you need to be a talented salesperson.

Are you an Incorporated or Limited Business?

Okay, now what about becoming an incorporated or limited company? With all the above business types, you can just add the label Incorporated, Limited or Corporation. These do offer some protection and I would certainly recommend it for certain types of professionals: lawyers, doctors, safety consultants, accountants, transportation and/or any industry where the advice or service you provide has the potential to affect a person in a negative way.

For any other industry, anyone can set up their business at any of the above designations at the start. However, look at the level of funds flowing through your company. Is there enough income to pay the higher fees related to incorporation? Often, it does not really pay to become incorporated until you earn at least over $80,000 a year in gross income. I suggest this threshold because of the extra costs involved. Filing taxes for an incorporated company ranges from $600-$2,000 per year which does not include the cost of monthly bookkeeping. Don't forget the annual filing costs through your lawyer. In general, there are a lot more hoops to jump through and extra regulations and expenses if you are incorporated. I do suggest that you look into it, regardless of your business structure. Speak with a lawyer and an accountant to understand if incorporation will benefit you or not.

It is very important to speak with an accountant because of all the recent changes with our Canadian tax system. Many of the tax benefits that come with operating under a corporation have been slowly disappearing. I cannot stress enough the importance of seeking the advice of an accountant and a lawyer prior to proceeding with incorporation. Get all the information you can.

Pros of Incorporating: Provides some liability protection (however, most suppliers will only deal with you if you personally sign off, thus negating the protection that incorporation previously provided). Under this model, you as the owner are now considered an employee of the corporation, the corporation pays most of the taxes and a corporation can have the appearance of being a more professional organization or a more legitimate business (although this is merely optics, some people feel it is worth the extra expense).

Cons to Incorporating: High costs, higher requirements for filing and paperwork, requiring a full team to support you such as a lawyer, an accountant and a bookkeeper.

Bottomline, any business can be a SEBO, a BAB or Limited (corporation) company. Be clear on where your strengths and weak-nesses lie as an entrepreneur. This will assist you in deciding which type of business you wish to run, as well as prepare you to deal with all aspects of your business.

What Type of Businessperson Are You?

Perhaps you are the type of business owner that understands the industry, sees a hole in the market and can create a service or a product to fill a need and know you yourself and perhaps a few others can build upon as a partnership. Or perhaps you would prefer to build a team to fill that need where you are, for the most part, hands off, and must hire staff to carry out the work. You are the salesperson or the face of your company.

Be clear on the type of businessperson you are and the business structure you excel in. This will be key in planning how to develop your business.

1.6 Stages of Business

"Failure is success, if we learn from it."
– Malcom Forbes

Having available cash to work with is crucial at every step of your business and each stage of business comes with its own financial challenges and decisions.

Did you pick up this book because the words "cash-flow" caught your attention? Every business owner's goal is to create cash—cash to run their company, cash to feed their families, cash to pay the bills, cash to keep a roof over your head, to do the work you love, to do what you are good at, cash to go on that dream vacation, or cash to attain a goal you have.

Most people start their own business to make a living their own way, to do something they love or something they are good at. If you have started a business, then I hope you have—and will continue to find—some useful tips throughout this book to ensure you can successfully keep doing what you love.

Liquidity: The Starting Key to a Successful Business

Cash flow comes down to "liquidity" also known as "available cash." The key to having a successful business is having available cash which allows you to stay on top of your expenses, plan for expansion, fix a crucial piece of equipment or replace equipment as needed. The ultimate goal is to have excess available cash, which is also known as "profit".

Many people start up a business, use all of their life savings and/ or go into debt to service their daily business over the first year. This is one of the most common flaws with cash flow within the start-up phase.

Even if you spent little on the start-up, it can take a while before your company gets stable footing in the marketplace. Then what?

Start Up Phase of Business

At the start-up phase, a business has a huge outlay in costs and very little cash flowing in. During this stage, not only will a business owner not have a wage, they still have their regular monthly living expenses for themselves and their family. The start-up phase is the planning stage where a business' framework is laid. The right framework is crucial for the long-term success of a business, yet this is also the learning stage for a business owner, where trial and error take place, where the strengths and weaknesses of an owner start making themselves very clear.

Hopefully, a new business owner will be open enough to hearing feedback. Business owners get into business for their great idea—their "sure thing"—believing they have the magic secret to success. Regardless of their magical product or service, a new business owner should consider joining a mastermind group, finding a mentor or speaking to other industry business owners to learn their pain points and how they overcame them.

There is often a lack of income for the owner for at least a year. When you are doing your planning, will you have other income sources to help cover your living expenses during this time? Will you have employment insurance for a few months? Do you have a spouse that can carry the monthly living costs? Do you have savings to cover you during this start-up phase? Plan to have a safety net for the costs of day-to-day living.

What types of upfront costs are part of starting up your business? Sit down and make a list and a plan. Consider the following:

- What do your competitors do that you feel you can do better? What will that look like?
- Do you want a web presence? Social media presence?
- Do you need equipment? How soon must the equipment be in place? Can you work with a cheaper version of equipment?
- Do you have a bookkeeper? Accountant? Lawyer?
- Are you incorporating or not incorporating?
- Does your line of work have a high potential for liability? If so, then incorporation may be the way to go.
- Do you require staff?

These are just some of the many questions you should answer before spending all of your life savings in the start-up phase. All of us would love to have the best tools, equipment and great top-notch staff to run our companies. However, can you make do with older or used equipment? Are there skilled persons that can help you out during the early stages? The less you spend upfront, the more working capital you have.

The Building Stage of Business

This is the stage on which many businesses get stuck, or worse, they have to close their doors. In this stage, you may need to focus on maintaining "working capital". If you need business loans to purchase newer equipment or fix the equipment you have, you may need investors, or if you need new and different equipment, need to hire specialized staff, a manager, HR person, or expand into a store-front location, all of these require capital investment or working capital before anyone else will work with you.

What I have seen firsthand is that the majority of business owners live paycheque to paycheque. They are so stretched and unable to pay for much-needed repairs or payroll. The reality is, we have all experienced working from paycheque to paycheque and it doesn't feel good. The increased stress on the owner affects the relationships around them—with their families, friends, suppliers. When a business owner is confident and has steps in place to address shortages, whether it is temporary or seasonally, this saves a lot of a business owner's sanity.

Every business owner faces a grind, "a lack of money and pure fatigue are usually the top reasons why business owners are ready to throw in the towel"[10] and closing the doors. "The average work week for an employee is 34.5 hrs, where for business owners 2 out of 3 exceed 40 hrs a week and 1 in 10 of those exceed a whopping 70 hours a week!"[11] This makes running a business no longer fun or exciting. As the stress grows, the spiral speeds up. That's right, the spiral—when an owner starts using debt, whether it is credit cards or personal lines of credit to pay staff, to pay monthly bills, the financial hole just gets deeper and deeper.

Most business owners have struggled with this. Some made it through the slow season and were able to pay their debts and start again. Many struggle from one payment to the next wondering if they will make it another month. This is when all non-essentials cease. Debts are owed everywhere.

Gabe's Seasonal Slumps

Gabe is a friendly, go-lucky guy. He is very welcoming and takes the time to visit with people; he is happy to share funny stories of the many odd encounters he experienced operating the locomotive. The stunning scenery is always changing. This was his bliss: being in nature and experiencing it at its best, and yes at times, at its worst.

---

[10] 3 Signs That You Should Shut Down Your Business – Deborah Mitchell, CEO & Founder, Deborah Mitchell Media Associates. https://www.entrepreneur.com/article/250267

[11] A fine Line: How Much Do Business Owners Work? https://www.boltinsurance.com/knowledge-center/infographics/

Gabe ended up asking for his family's help to tide him over his business' seasonal slump—people only wanted to travel in the spring to fall seasons which made the winters tough. Often, Gabe was unable to pay his regular payments so his family was integral in getting him by until he could build his business.

Can you relate to Gabe? Have you experienced similar situations? Hats off to you if you were well prepared and planned for slowdowns! Unfortunately, most people get caught up in debt and start spinning, or they go to family for "temporary" financial aid, or perhaps a couch to sleep on.

If you manage to get through the business building stage, there is the next stage: Survival. How do you continue running your business each day without "burnout"?

Survival Stage of Business

At this stage, you made it through the first year. It's still a struggle but now you need to expand, hire more staff, get professionals in place, upgrade your equipment, or at the very least, you will need to maintain your equipment just to keep up with demand.

Perhaps you want to advertise more or look at what is your ideal limit. Are you able to keep up with the current demands? This is when you start to really look at whether you are making money or losing money. You must ask yourself, is this worth it? Can I take time off, am I able to work long hours? There are new questions and new revelations. Or maybe things are running along adequately and you are happy with where you are and do not wish to grow. Many sole proprietors are in this boat, month to month.

At each stage of your business, there is an obvious need for cash flow for the reasons we have mentioned. One of my favourite people with whom I've work is a gentleman I will call Fred. Fred and his wife, Jana, struggled to start up a transportation business, starting with one bus.

Jana continued to work full-time at her job. It had benefits and she became the main supporter of the family while Fred built up his business as a bus driver in his own company. Transportation businesses fall under federal laws so there is heavy paperwork that needs attention regularly and strict regulations that needs following.

At first, Jana was the bookkeeper and ran payroll as well as working full-time at her other job. Then they needed a dispatch office and a waiting area for passengers. Jana and Fred had to remortgage their home to get by and all the money Fred made went back into the business. As the business grew, they hired a number of extra bus drivers, back-up dispatch people and staff to help load passengers' luggage into the busses. In a short amount of time, two people on payroll grew to 18 people! This included a regular bookkeeper to provide a break for Jana, who was exhausted with all her extra tasks on top of working full-time.

Fred was inundated with so many fees, registrations and paperwork that he was so glad that his head dispatcher took on that role as well. I worked with Fred and Jana through their start-up phase and during a lot of their growth. They were great people to work with and always wanted to do a good job for their staff, which was greatly appreciated.

Like Gabe, available cash flow for Fred was tight. I was preparing payments for items that had to be paid, then asking which bills were more of a priority as we had few funds leftover. We would circulate the bills, making payments on the larger ones, and kept on top of the bills required for running day-to-day operations like fuel costs, hydro, phone and payroll. We also had to ensure money was available for their loans and investors.

I had the weekly task of juggling who needed paying and what we could pay. I would provide Fred and Jana with a list of options, cheques attached to each bill, asking Fred, "Well, we have $35,000 in the bank, payroll comes out in two days. Insurance and utilities will be covered. Now, which creditors can we pay with the remaining $10,000?"

The list of creditors always surprised him. He would laugh and say, "I owe that much?" Fred always seemed very nonchalant about what he owed.

My reply, "This week, yes, but next week we will need another $22,000 and we still do not have enough to make payroll. We would need another $51,000 just to catch up. These are the 'must pay now' bills!"

Fred had to make tough decisions about who to pay, about when and what could be delayed. They were always using their lines of credit and available funds were dwindling fast. I will return to Fred and Jana later to share some of the key things they did well. Here, I just wanted to note some of the challenges that frequently occur as a business grows.

In all businesses, "lack of cash flow" is all too real. In this book, my goal is to help you succeed in your business by explaining some of the "money-glitches" that either myself or a fellow business owner has stumbled over. I hope to provide you with a plan so you can avoid contending with these issues in your business.

2. CREATING A POSITIVE CASH FLOW

All the tasks you do as a business owner are either making you money or saving you money. Break down your daily tasks into those two baskets. Also, do you, yourself need to handle a task or can you delegate the task to someone else? Remember that your skill is what makes you money and that is why you started your business. It is easy to get pulled away from your focus to attend to tasks that seem interesting and useful. Surfing the web may be fun and interesting, but is it making you money or is it saving you money? Again, if it is not in one of those two baskets, then revaluate your daily tasks.

I recently met a lovely artist on one of my trips to Montreal. Kah is quite an entrepreneur. She incorporates real-life stories of the person she is painting, overlaying articles about them to create a beautiful interplay within her portraits.

I stopped to admire her art and we started up a conversation about how, for years, she was an employee of Xerox but her love for art finally drew her into a very different lifestyle.

At first, her focus was solely on paintings and getting them into galleries for the exposure. It can be very difficult for an artist to get the attention and approval to show in a gallery, and when they do, at least 50 to 70% of a piece's purchase price goes to the gallery. The other issue for artists is that they have a limited market. A price tag of $2000 and up for a one-of-a-kind painting means there is only a slim sector of people who both value art and can afford the work.

There is nothing wrong with this, however, the phrase "starving artist" is common for a reason. Kah decided to take the bull by the horns and diversify. With a single painting, she created prints in metal or canvas at a price range of $300-1000 (depending on size). She also printed her paintings onto handbags and computer bags. The price range for these was $30-80, an affordable price range for someone who liked her art but had a limited budget.

With one painting, she was able to hit several different markets and have her paintings showcased at craft fairs, artist fairs and galleries.

She then took it a step further and invested in her home, creating a beautiful and welcoming gallery space showcasing her and another artist's work. By doing this, she saved paying the commissions that would normally go to a gallery. Plus, she would receive the commissions from showing the other artist's work. Investing in yourself is key, whether that is taking courses or putting money into something to get a better rate of return. In this case, she invested in her home.

Kah still showed her work in other galleries from time to time, for the exposure or to show her more unique paintings, but her focus was building her business by increasing her available markets. In turn, this increases her sales because she has many sources of income doing the one skill she loved.

This artist also wrote a book about leaving the comfort of a successful career in an international business to becoming an artist doing what she loves every day. She writes about the process and why she took the leap. I was blessed to meet such a positive, beautiful individual and I wish her and all artists the best in their artistic endeavours. And yes, I did indeed purchase a computer bag from Kah with a beautiful print of Marilyn Monroe with red butterflies, some of my favorite things. I would love to invest in one of her paintings in the future.

2.1 Problem Solving Is a Business

If you can solve problems for others,
you will always be able to make money.

Every business idea first started out as the intention to make other's lives better through a skill, product or service. An entrepreneur discovers a need and feels they are the one with the best solution. The more specialized your business, the more you are sought after. Have you heard of the 80/20 rule? It is this: 20% of what you offer often provides 80% of your income.

Let's go back to Johnny for a moment. Johnny was looking at providing a new service to clients, providing mechanical assistance for getting their vehicle if they were stuck. A typical client for this service might be a woman who has little to no experience with fixing their own vehicle, including how to change a tire.

Johnny saw this growing need due to the many phone calls he would receive from his current customers asking for assistance. Yes, a tow truck could be called, however, they explicitly trusted Johnny, their mechanic, to work on their vehicle. He was honest in what they needed and charged the expected rates. His clientele was built on trust. The clients felt they were treated fairly and that he always maintained their vehicles well. These clients trust Johnny's expertise and integrity.

Due to his reputation, clients would call Johnny in the mornings, asking for assistance if their car could not start or if they had a flat tire. Johnny would drive over in his pickup truck and help them out.

This is just one example about how entrepreneurs discover a new service or product which provides value to others, value that others are happy to pay for. When we discover new ways to provide a solution to a problem, then we can monetize it. I know Johnny's clients were more than happy to pay for his time!

One of my other clients, Todd, specializes in floor laying. He is extremely knowledgeable and able to do any type of flooring. This is where the bulk of his money is made. He then decided to try a hand at home construction. The building was beautiful, well made and he had no problem taking on this project. However, the nature of home construction involves payments at intermittent intervals. Often, these intervals were inconsistent and would be held up until someone was able to verify the right steps and applicable permits were in place.

For a small company with staff and little savings set aside, it was hard to find more projects to keep his staff working while the big project was held up and payments from the big project would not come in on time to cover payroll. As the company's bookkeeper, I saw their struggles firsthand and know that if he had set aside at least six months of wages and expenses prior to working on the building project, he would have been fine. However, this set him back quite a bit. In the end, the construction project that took up 120% of his time generated less than 10% profit.

Eventually, my client decided to go back to only flooring as it was what brought in the most money and he knew he would be succes-sful. Sometimes changing and adding services can be detrimental to your business, especially when the terms and conditions are different, rules are unfamiliar or expectations unclear. Without a lot of experience, taking on a new service can be a steep—and unprofitable—learning curve.

What problem do you solve for your clients? Ensure you are specific about your solutions. Look at your list of services/products: how much money can you charge for each item? What is the profit margin for each one? Are you too diversified? Should you offer a few items or specialize in only one?

The most successful businesses for which I have worked avoid spreading themselves too thin. They focus on doing one or two things extremely well. It's something to consider, especially when first starting your business.

2.2 Building Value for Your Clients

*Providing information and tips to your clients for free will help
position yourself as an expert in your field.*

This also enables clients to solve their problems for themselves which many people appreciate. Most people take pride in the ability to do things on their own, especially if it will save them money. Now, this may seem like you are giving away your services for free and, yes, perhaps you are, initially. However, by doing this, you are providing education and advocating for your clients. Remember, the key here is positioning yourself as an expert in your field.

On the Advice of a Pro

I, myself, walked into our local building supply store and started asking questions about how to tile my floor. The employee assisting me was so helpful and generous in explaining what I needed to do. He even specified that the cement needed for sticking the tile to the floor must have the consistency of peanut butter. His tip made my resulting tile job look professional. I felt pride in doing this small job myself, a feeling that was important to me.

When people ask me which building supply store to use, I always direct them to that wonderful store where the staff was so helpful. Now, I am sure that they did not make a lot of money off me, their target market is the large construction companies, the tiling contractors that need a lot of material. I am a side market only, but you can bet that when or if I build a home, I suggest that my contractor deal with that building supply company. This is what "building value" means.

When potential clients see you as an expert, then they will think of you first when the time comes that advice is not enough to solve their problem. Then you can charge as per usual to assist them.

By providing tips and free consultation, you have accomplished several key factors in doing business well: Firstly, (and most importantly), you have identified your target market. Secondly, you have created a client base willing to potentially to hire you over your competition. All by simply sharing your expertise for free.

My dear friend, Wilma, is a mortgage broker who offers free sessions on how to rebuild your credit. She provides the key indicators that banks and credit unions look for to approve you for a mortgage. When Wilma's session participants are ready to apply for a mortgage, guess who they will seek out first?

Wilma takes this a step further. She has aligned herself with other industry professionals in mortgage, like bankers and other insurance brokers. Together, they will do presentations, seminars or webinars on all the ins and outs of getting into your first home. With home ownership's constantly changing rules, these sessions are valuable. In this model, you may not feel like you have gained any new clients at first, and quite frankly, you may not see the pay-off for years. In Wilma's case, a home is a big purchase and it takes time for people to get their ducks in a row, save money, define what they need/want in a home and approach the professionals.

Providing free education to the general public is part of building your business for the long term. Also, when one-time customers or prior participants of a free seminar, workshop or webinar, are ready to take the next step, they are already pre-qualified potential buyers and they are likely thinking of you! This is likely one of the biggest hurdles for business owners—getting in front of their target market.

2.3 Value Yourself and Your Business

Only when we value our business will others invest in ours.

Value your business FIRST! Know that you are providing a service or a product in which you yourself trust. We are our business' best salesperson so by exuding confidence in our own service or product, others will view it in that same light.

Put Your Money Where Your Mouth Is

One key practice of valuing your business is putting aside a percentage of your profits first. This is like "paying yourself first" with your personal finances and setting aside money for retirement. Similarly, setting aside a set percentage of profit before you deal with expenses is key. Start with 5% and increase that amount until you can put aside 10-15% of your profits each year.

Why is this so important? Setting money aside earmarked specifically as your business' emergency fund will be your saving grace from increasing your business' debt. As you may have already experience, it is getting more and more difficult to qualify for business loans when there are downturns in the economy. Wouldn't it be amazing to have your own emergency funds to get you through the difficult times?

Consider this practice as investing in your own business. If you do not value what your business offers and are not willing to invest into your own business, why would a bank or an investor put their funds into your business? The same can be said for our clients. If I am not regularly investing in myself by continually staying on top of trends, changes with the tax laws or reporting changes, how can I best service my clients? Chances are good they will find someone who can help them out more.

If you watch *Dragon's Den*, you'll notice that most presenters have already invested financially in their product or service; they are on the show to seek external investment and mentorship to take their business to the next level. It's the judges' jobs to gauge whether the entrepreneurs presenting have a business idea that will succeed with their involvement. The judges on *Dragon's Den* are experienced business owners who have managed to learn how to succeed. Through many past business failures, they have risen up again with great success, learning key tools and now have the right connections in place. This has enabled them to shine as experts who can now show others the way or the best potential track for success.

The experience they have gained from their many ventures is why others seek them out. Their expertise allows them to spot whether or not a business has strong potential for success. I must say, however, that, just like the *Dragon's Den* judges, even the investment of your own money, blood, sweat and tears into your business may not always result in success.

Invest Wisely In Your Equipment

Another area where companies do not value themselves is regarding the equipment they use to run their business. As we all know, there is often a large cash outlay for equipment. Yes, you can write off a portion of the expense annually for several years on your income statement. This is a great practice, but you should also put the value of those funds (the portion being depreciated) aside for capital investment. Whatever amount you write off for the piece of equipment, it has a replacement value.

The government keeps a current estimate for how long your equipment should last and how long you can expect to be able to write it off as an expense— basically until the value of the equipment is "nil". Therefore, the amount which you set aside for future capital investment should at least equal the amount written off each year. This way, even if costs go up for replacing your equipment, you now at least have a large down payment and/or a much smaller loan request. Financial institutions love when you only request a percentage of your equipment's value! This means you have equity, also a term they love.

As a bookkeeper, my tools are my computers and the programs I use, which require upgrading annually. Quite frankly, each year the programs are bigger and require more space on my computer, which in turn, often requires I upgrade to a faster computer. Nothing is worse than waiting for a simple entry to post, waiting long enough to have a cup of coffee means there are issues needing to be addressed. Yes, a bookkeeper's nightmare and an inefficient use of time. I have little patience for that, and my clients certainly are not interested in paying me to drink a pot of coffee while waiting on only 20 transactions!

I always have two running computers so that if one goes down, I do not lose any time; I can use my back up computer while the main one is being fixed. In saying that, I once had the unfortunate case of both of my computers going down in the same week with different issues. This slowed my output for a week. My solution was having three computers, which I rotate for upgrading.

The keys here are: invest a percentage into a business savings fund and set aside funds to replace aging equipment.

2.4 Invoicing & Payment Options

The length of time it takes to send a bill, the customer will take
two to three times longer to get around to paying you!

One of the biggest problems a small business may face is getting paid on time. Since 80% of our economy is made up of small businesses, there is a large percentage of businesses which operate on limited cash resources from time to time.

A traditional business model is one where you provide a service and only get paid once the service is complete. This is fine, however, if you are a dryer repairman, for example, you need to provide the invoice upon completion of the work before leaving the premises and expect payment before leaving.

It's no use doing work if you are not going to get paid for it. As soon as the work is finished, leave your invoice with your customer or send your invoice out right away. Do not extend credit unless necessary. If the account is not paid within the normal payment terms, don't be afraid to send a letter or statement reminding your customer that the account is due with your company's terms for late payment fees. The average percentage charged for late fees is 1.5% per month when not received within 30 days. Also, ensure that these terms are clearly and prominently written on every invoice.

Your time, your products, and/or your services are very valuable and they come at a cost. So to avoid unintentional pro-bono work, expect payment for your service and make this clear in your payment terms.

Let's say you are the dryer repairman. You have completed your work and take your leave, saying to your customer that the secretary or bookkeeper will send the bill. This can work if you ensure that is done as soon as you get back to the office. The more prompt the bill, the more likely you will get a prompt payment without having to send reminders. The key here is that the longer it takes you to bill your customer, the more your customer believes that it is not important to pay right away. The rule of thumb here is: the length of time it takes you to send a bill, it might take two to three times longer for the customer to pay you. How long can you afford to wait for your customers' payments?

The computer network professional that services one of the offices for which I work is notorious for sending invoices very late. Upon starting work with this company, I had to deal with a slew of invoices from up to three years previous from the IT contractor. This was quite frustrating because I had to review three years of records to see if any payments had already been issued for these invoices. Then I had to review the invoices that were billed to ensure they were not duplicates. Once I verified that there were no payments made and that these were certainly owing, I then had to verify the work was actually done! In addition, the IT employee involved in the billed work was no longer with the company so it was even more difficult to verify the invoices. Thankfully, the equipment billed was there and working, so the office did end up paying all the invoices. What are the legal ramifications of late invoice remittance?

There are some general guidelines around this so I will share these rules. If you do not have a contract with a vendor which specifically states that the vendor must send an invoice within a specific time period, the vendor may still be able to send an invoice despite the delay, even much later.

The two potential defenses to a late invoice are: Firstly, the normal timeframe for a vendor to sue on an unpaid invoice would be two years after the payment was due. However, if there is a signed contract, the invoice can be expected to be paid up to or four years after the payment was due!

Be aware that the clock starts as soon as the materials or goods were provided, even if an invoice was not. Also, if you know that the goods and services were indeed provided, you are still on the hook for it. If the case is that you are unaware of goods or services were provided, you will need to provide details or back up to that point to prove this may be the case.

Video footage can be used to determine if goods or services were indeed provided or not. One example that has made the rounds on the internet is video footage of a delivery person supposedly dropping off an Amazon package. This video footage shows the delivery person coming to the door, putting the package down at the door, then filling out the details of the package on his handheld computer. The delivery person then picks up the package and takes it back with him to his truck! In this case, video footage provided the consumer with evidence when approaching Amazon about their package. Due diligence, and checks and balances in place are key.

As a service provider, be firm and clearly identify your expectations on your payment terms before you start the work. If things do not go as planned, concentrate your focus on preserving the relationship you have built. If your customer or client has legitimate complaints, then don't hesitate to fix the problems. This is where having customer service skills will make the difference.

Excellent Customer Service Skills is always Key

Have you evaluated yourself on your customer service? Consider the following and please ask others or your current clients for help with this:

- What are your customer service strengths?
- Do people like engaging with you? Do you give credit or praise easily? And why?
- What customer experiences have you enjoyed that you can apply to your own business?

Let's be real, not everyone is a people person and not everyone is an extrovert.

When we get real with our abilities—our strong characteristics and our weak attributes—only then can we surround ourselves with a team of people who possess the strengths which a business requires.

The book, *Think and Grow Rich* by Napoleon Hill, lists many examples of how successful business owners surround themselves with others who are experts in different fields like human resources, sales, administration, or law. A business owner's lack of knowledge is offset by bringing in people who know these things. *Think and Grow Rich* is a good read with lots of great takeaways.

2.5 Monitoring Your Accounts Receivables

As the business owner, all the risk is on you,
therefore minimize that risk.

We, as business owners, often enjoy what we do and believe in our skills, which is why we are confident charging for them. Let's look at the risk level of providing services and the potential issues with not being paid for them! We all went into business to make money, not to lose our shirt or our homes. Yet, receivables and collection are a common issue among businesses.

With every business, the service costs are usually the costs of labour—wages, government deductions and benefits. Then there are the products we purchase for resale to customers. This is usually the highest costs of outlay because we want to provide customers with options. There are also general overhead costs that are not directly billable like rent and utilities, vehicle costs, freight and postage, costs of software, costs to maintain or purchase equipment. Finally, there are cost for experts such as accountants, book-keepers, lawyers, and/or IT.

As a business owner, all the risk is on you, including if any of your staff or accountants make an error. You are responsible for getting broken equipment fixed and/or pay fines. That's right, you as the business owner, are responsible for other's mistakes.

It is important to ensure your customers pay in a timely fashion so you can maintain a positive cash flow for the expenses above. Delinquency costs money. You are carrying another person's debt. As well, putting money out for the products or paying your staff to do the work is carrying them, too. If your business is not a bank, then extending credit to customers only puts your company at risk.

Here is an example: Customer X owes you $15,000 which is 65 days overdue. You then have incurred the following costs:

administrative time to send invoices, follow up with phone calls, costs of generating invoices and mailing them. The average cost per invoice[12] being sent out is $8.44 per invoice, each time. This includes the labour involved.

Assuming there is at least three letters or invoices being sent out during this period (initial, after 30 days, after 60 days), that is 3 x $8.44 = $25.32 for one customer! Could you imagine if you have 20 customers in this position? This would cost you additional $506.40 in extra time to chase down receivables.

The Cost of Lost Opportunity

Lost opportunity costs is calculating the amount of lost potential of generating additional income on money owed. There is a formula that calculates potential loss on that money, and conversely, help you figure out what you could have made instead.

If money owed was actually in an investment earning a potential interest of 6% for you, then use the following calculation in the example below:

[(Accounts Receivable x Rate of return)/365] x days sales outstanding

Let's look at the balance owed by one customer:
[(15,000 x 6%) / 365] x 65 = $160.27 in lost opportunity.

Now look at the payment terms of your suppliers. They may require you pay in 30 days. If you allow your customer to pay you within 45 to 60 days, this now creates a cash flow gap in your bank account of about 15 days!

So now, your customer invoice becomes:

---

[12]The True Cost Of Carrying Accounts Receivable.
https://www.creditmgtgroup.com/2017-03-10-the-true-cost-of-carrying-accounts-receivable

Added costs of your time and expense in chasing it down: $25.32 plus the lost opportunity costs: $160.27. And this is if you are paid within 65 days from the initial invoice being sent out! The longer it takes to be paid for work you completed, costs go up. This does not even take into account the time and expenses to provide the service/product for your customer.

There is also the risk of bad debt, in other words, not getting paid at all for a product or service you provided. With the constant changes in the economy and increased competition, bad debts can really affect your business, not just in the loss of payment and in your time chasing down payments, but in the amount of sales needed to recover the loss of capital! If you have a profit margin of 10% on a $1,000 bad debt, you would need to sell $10,000 worth of product or service to recover from that one loss.

So, how do you get your customers to pay on time?

Bottomline, requiring payment upfront is the most successful way to ensure you are paid. If you are in an industry in which the product and/or service are part of the total invoice, suggesting a portion of the bill is paid upfront prior to ordering items will help, especially over a certain value amount. At the very least, upfront payments may cover your restocking charges if the customer decides not to move forward with you.

Every industry operates differently but offering incentives for your customers so they provide payment in the early stages will go a long way in protecting your cash flow. Find a balance of being proactive while preserving your client relationship.

Perhaps you need to instill a late payment charge on bills not paid within a certain time frame. For example, ensure a note about payment terms—say, 30 days—is included on the invoice. Or perhaps provide an incentive for early payment, like 5% off if paid within 15 days. My clients loved this incentive when I applied it to them as 5% is a nice kick back. It covers the cost of GST and 5% can add up.

What payment options do you offer?

I recently attended a Xero conference, (Xero is bookkeeping online software) at which they provided statistics from a study on the length of time it takes to receive payment from customers. Here are the results of that study:

1. If you send an invoice via mail, it takes an average of 42 days to receive payment.

2. When invoices were sent online or provided right away, the time of payment was only 24 days.

3. When invoices were sent online, with immediate payment options, payment only takes 10 days!

By offering a variety of payment options, specifically online ones, it was much easier and faster to receive payment. The more convenient you make it for customers, the higher the likelihood of receiving payment. You can also consider mobile payment solutions such as Square or Apple Pay which are great options for smaller businesses. Compare the fees involved in offering all these payment options and shop around. Remember, these expenses are a normal cost of doing business and if this allows you to receive payments from your customers in a timely fashion, then it is more than worth it! I will discuss payment options in detail in Chapter 2.4.

The above steps are usually successful for receiving payment from your customer. However, there are some situations that become difficult, therefore, the next step would be to pick up the phone and call your customer. This should be done after the 45-

day mark (just in case, there was a delay in the payment being sent).

Make direct contact in a positive and friendly way. A voice and conversation go a long way in keeping the process civil. During your phone call, offer options or a payment plan for collecting the funds. Let's say you have sent out notices—the first one included 5% off if paid in 30 days. However, the bill is due and payable within 30 days so now you are charging 1.5% interest for each month the customer is delinquent. You have made nice phone call reminders and offered various payment terms, but if you are still not getting a response, I would suggest sending email reminders with their options and any incentive you could provide. After several months, perhaps provide them with a one-time offer to reverse all late fees if they pay within the next 14 days.

When contacting them, remember that we all have unexpected, temporary setbacks; see what can be done to provide a "win-win" situation for both parties.

When both parties feel good about the end result, not only have you provided a bridge in working with your customer, your customer will be more likely to use your services again in the future. You have treated them like a human being.

Although you may have made every effort to work with your customer to receive payment, you might not always succeed in collecting the funds. After a year of attempts, the remaining two options you have are: write it off as bad debt or work with a credit company that specializes in recovering bad debts. They do take a fee (a percentage) of the total funds they recover but it's better than not getting paid at all.

Do remember that for any customers who are still unable to pay their debts, make sure your write these off on the books, otherwise you will be required to remit sales taxes on amounts you never received!

2.6 Costs Involved in Getting New Clients

*"It costs five times as much to attract a new customer
than to keep an existing one." – Khalid Saleh*

If you have been in business for a while, you may remember the time it took as well as the effort and money you spent in advertising. What are the costs involved in getting new clients?

According to a study done by the Invesp,[13] it costs five times as much to attract a new customer than it takes to keep an existing one. In their survey, Invesp found that 44% of companies focus on getting new clients, whereas only 18% focus on keeping their current ones. If it costs five times as much to get a new client and 44% of companies focus on getting new clients, they must be spending a lot of extra funds for little return.

The 18% of companies that focused on keeping their existing clients spend far less on expenses and are far more successful. Customer loyalty and retention start with their initial impression, but it is ongoing service that keeps them coming back. The probability of selling to an existing customer is 60 to 70%[14] whereas the probability of selling to a new customer is only 5-20%. Can you see the value in retaining your existing customers?

One other key statistic is that by increasing customer retention by only 5%, you may see an increase 25% to 95% in your profits. Sounds a lot like the 80/20 rule we discussed previously, the rule is that 20% of your clients results in 80% of your business income.

So, how do you keep customers for the long haul?

---

[13] Customer Acquisition Vs. Retention Costs – Statistics and Trends. Khalid Saleh -https://www.invespcro.com/blog/customer-acquisition-retention/

[14] Customer Acquisition Vs. Retention Costs – Statistics and Trends, Khalid Saleh -https://www.invespcro.com/blog/customer-acquisition-retention/

Tip One: Stay on top of new trends and technology.

For some, keeping up with trends and technology may be a challenge, but it also may make your business as efficient as possible. In the past 10 years of my industry, new apps have emerged that can automatically send information to your bookkeeper on a daily basis. Mundane tasks are now automated and both owners and bookkeepers can see what is happening on a regular basis with shared, online access. This has also allowed the bookkeeper to become an integral part of a business and allow them to provide valuable tips in real time.

Tip Two: Provide face-to-face, personal customer service.

Do you measure the customer satisfaction level of your clients? A *Forbes* magazine article identified a "worrisome" statistic that stated, "60-80% of customers who describe themselves as satisfied do not go back to do more business with the company that initially satisfied them."[15] They found that there was a lack of connection, missing a human face or voice.

Loyalty is built through relationships and with everything being available online, there is limited relationship-building when it is based upon clicks, it is just as easy to click onto another site with the next best offer. Yes, we need to use tools available to us so we can provide better service and there is fierce competition for customer attention. Implement innovative marketing strategies which include more of a relationship focus.

Building rapport is important for any business in any market and is achievable through various methods. A quick text to check in on your customer, an email offering a free subscription for tips you share with your loyal customers, a congratulations on the

---

[15] Acquiring New Customers Is Important, But Retaining Them Accelerates Profitable Growth. Larry Myler - https://www.forbes.com/sites/larrymyler/2016/06/08/acquiring-new-customers-is-important-but-retaining-them-accelerates-profitable-growth/#7db929f16671

birth of their new baby, these are simple yet effective personal touches.

Third Tip: Utilize Digital Methods of Customer Acquisition

There are many ways to reach out to your audience each day and these tools are at your disposal. The first key, match which tool to use for connecting with your clients based upon your target market, and secondly, or most importantly, keep a conversation going.

You can focus on acquiring new customers but the likelihood that a new customer will follow through with a purchase is 5-20%, whereas there is a 50% likelihood of an existing customer trying new products from you. Return customers also spend up to 31% more in comparison to new customers[16].

Younger generations, such as Gen Z to millennials, are glued to their mobile devices. If you are not advertising in some way that is accessible[17] through these devices, it will be very hard to break into that market. Staying current is crucial. If your market is these generations, hiring a social media savvy person to manage your social media, web, and mobile presence is an ideal way to learn how to connect with your market and what appeals to them.

I recently had a great conversation with a landscaper named Josh. Josh has owned his own landscaping business for many years. He has a fleet of vehicles and a large staff to address the many needs of his customers. Josh had a young family when he started, and he invested a lot of time and money into his business.

---

[16] Customers And Start Growing The Ones You Have, Jeff Pruitt, chairman and CEO of tallwave. https://www.inc.com/jeff-pruitt/why-your-businesss-growth-potential-isnt-in-net-new.html

[17] Acquiring New Customers Is Important, But Retaining Them Accelerates Profitable Growth. Larry Myler -
https://www.forbes.com/sites/larrymyler/2016/06/08/acquiring-new-customers-is-important-but-retaining-them-accelerates-profitable-growth/#7db929f16671

They had their struggles in the beginning but these days, he is still very busy and is in a far more comfortable position.

I asked Josh if he is able to keep up with new customers. He said he does not pick up any new customers anymore as he has had a regular, stable base for many years. He has found it easier to maintain his current customer base. This was an interesting revelation so I probed more.

Josh went on to explain that with each new client, a lot of time was spent establishing expectations and how best to meet their needs. It took up a lot of personal time addressing each new client individually until he found what they needed. To balance this, Josh found that new clients weren't worth attracting for two reasons: he had to be more competitive with his rates to land a new client, and he was always at a loss for the first year until his company could prove itself.

For Josh, it just did not make sense to take a loss *and* take time away from his current clientele. That lack of attention to current clients potentially put those relationships at risk. As well, servicing his regular, loyal customers at their rates did not set him up for a loss. By keeping his rates consistent, he has employed a great group of staff that have been with him for years and he was still making money.

For Josh's business, taking on new customers means expanding, more training, and a lot more work with the chance of accidently losing good customers due to lack of attention.

Josh had reached a point in his business where his processes and strategies were working. They were making him money without burning him out like it did in the building stages of his company. He was at a point in his business that was steady, his customers were regular, and things were easy. There was no desire to change. For Josh, and for many business owners, if it ain't broke, don't fix it.

There comes a time in every business when you need to evaluate whether or not you have met your goals. Perhaps you want to grow and expand? Or perhaps you would rather shrink to a manageable size? A key to success is identifying where you would like to be and what you would like to achieve.

2.7 Taking Care of Your Customers & Inventory

*Inventory can your greatest asset and
your greatest liability at the same time.*

When I shop, I prefer having options in size and colour and love touching and feeling a product. This experience is one many people look for when shopping. For some companies, your inventory may be your main source of income, therefore it is an asset. However, the longer an item is taking up shelf or floor space, the bigger the liability it becomes; you have locked up potentially available cash in your inventory.

There are calculations that can let you know if your inventory is sitting too long and calculate how much money is tied up into it.[18] Dealing with inventory is difficult— because you may have to order your inventory many months in advance, you are guessing at what trends will sell the next season.

What if the new trends take off and you cannot fill the number of potential orders? Can you partner with larger companies which stock more? If so, you can do one of two things, send your customer to them (great customer service) or you can let them know you will order it in for them.

Inventory is a necessity, but if it is not monitored well, you can be missing out on potential sales, or lose money on sitting inventory. Hopefully you do not have inventory sitting so long that you could open a museum!

---

[18]Days in Inventory https://financeformulas.net/Days-in-Inventory.html

Some quick tips:

- A good Point of Sale system (POS) will be crucial to your success in monitoring and sorting out your inventory. This is such a key piece of equipment for any retail store.
- Stock what sells: monitor what is selling and order more of that.

- Get rid of dead stock: make it a loss leader where it becomes a freebie, put it in a grab bag or donate it to good causes.

- Try to keep up with the trends but be aware, if you have too many similar items in your store, they may not sell. Also, if all the competitors carry the same stock, your stock may end up as dead stock.

- Are you able to purchase items in bulk? Can you work with another local-ish store to buy in larger quantities to save money?

I love how in the movie *Miracle on 34th Street* (the original 1947 version which I finally watched only this past year) the Santa Claus for the competing company was sending many of the parents and families to other stores that had particular items in stock, even if the prices were cheaper. In the movie's time period, such a practice was unheard of and there was initially a lot of opposition from the store's executives.

Then suddenly, the executives realized that their sales went up, despite sending customers elsewhere. This was a *eureka* moment for the executives—they found that part of providing good customer service was letting their potential customers know if other stores carried the same items or if it was cheaper elsewhere!

This is true customer service. Let's face it, we cannot meet everyone's needs nor are we able to make everyone happy. Making the needs of the customer more important than a momentary sale is a valuable service to customers. They may, in turn, come back to your store to do their shopping because they know your company has the customer's interest at heart.

I am not an inventory specialist so if you are looking for one, I would suggest locating a bookkeeper or accountant with experience dealing with inventory controls. They may have great ideas about best industry standards and tips for your company.

2.8 The Paradox of Choice[19]

"Less is More."
— Robert Browning

If you wish to grow your business quickly, look at what items in your business make you money. Really drill down with all your current income sources and figure out how much money is made in which category. You will find it amazing that 20% of your time produces 80% of your results, just like 80% of your sales will come from 20% of your activities/sales.

So, what makes those 20% of your sales or services so desirable? What are the characteristics that draw your customers to that 20%? Truly sit and identify each of your products/services specific traits. Make the same list for the sales and service that bring in 80% of your income. Compare the two lists, then pare down your business offerings to the items that actually make you money. Spend more time on the 80% and less time on the items that only produce 20% of your overall income. For some, this means specializing, or perhaps your list has revealed that your existing specialization is actually resulting in the bulk of your income (the 80%). If so, this is easy!

Another way to look at the 80/20 rule: 80% of your income comes from 20% of your customers. When there is a clear minority creating a majority, this is called the *Pareto Principle*.[20]

The *Pareto Principle* can be applied in a number of ways. There are business examples, such as 20% of employees are responsible for 80% of a company's output, or 20% of customers are

---

[19] The Paradox Of Choice: Why More Is Less By Barry Schwartz. https://www.goodreads.com/book/show/10639.The_Paradox_of_Choice

[20] Pareto Principle: The Statement, Explanation, Examples, Applications https://thefactfactor.com/life_skill/life_changing_principles/pareto-principle/761/

responsible for 80% of the revenues. Keep in mind these are not hard rules and the ratio will not always be exactly 80/20.

By reviewing key metrics, you should be able to find 80/20 ratios in your sales, your expenses and your staffing. By knowing the 20% of sales or services that brings in 80% of your income, you can implement strategies to maximize your income potential.

In some cases, you should keep the products or services that generate the most income (the 20%) and drop the rest (the 80%), or drop the products and services which only provide marginal benefits.

Another way you can look at this: Allocate your time wisely by working on the parts of the business which your core skills can improve significantly and leave the tasks outside of your skillset to other people. Work hardest on elements that work hardest for you. Reward the best employees well, cull the worst.

Similarly, drop the bad clients and focus on upselling and improving services to the best clients. The 80-20 Principle has the potential to multiply the profitability and effectiveness of any organization or individual.

"The value of the Pareto Principle for a manager is that it reminds you to focus on the 20 percent that matters. Of the things you do during your day, only 20 percent really matter. Those 20 percent produce 80 percent of your results. Identify and focus on those things. When the fire drills of the day begin to sap your time, remind yourself of the 20 percent you need to focus on. If something in the schedule must slip, if something isn't going to get done, make sure it's not part of that 20 percent".[21]

Looking at your daily habits on a micro level, you can find plenty of examples where the 80/20 Rule applies. You probably make most of your phone calls to a very small number of contacts stored in your phone. You likely spend a large chunk of your

---

[21]Pareto Principle – The 80-20 Rule – Complete Information. http://www.gassner.co.il/pareto/

money on a few things (perhaps rent, mortgage payments or food). There is a good chance that you spend most of your time with only a few people from the entire pool of people you know.

There is nothing wrong with looking for new customers, but don't forget the old ones. Keep in touch with your current clients as they are often a great source of referrals for potential new business. It's a fact that you can build a successful business around a smaller number of satisfied customers by simply providing them with excellent service and excellent products.

Loyal customers will always be "good money in the bank". They are easier to work with because they know how you operate and how you like things done. It's far less expensive to keep those long-term customers happy than it is to find new customers.

In Johnny's case, he has a very loyal group of customers which he wanted to ensure he continued to meet their needs to serve them the best he could. So his idea of adding mobile services to his already successful mechanic business is a good example of how he was focusing on his current clientele.

2.9 Value the Difficult Customer or Client

Build bridges and establish relationships that last.
The more satisfied and loyal your clients are,
the greater your cash flow will be.

Everyone has "good" clients as well as "tough" clients. Good clients pay on time and feel they are getting what they need. Tough clients are continually requiring more. They constantly have a concern or an issue and/or will hold back paying their fees until their needs are met. Tough clients are more likely seen as a burden, however if you can stop and really hear what they are saying, they can provide valuable information!

First off, they are letting you know there is a problem. If your product or service is substandard—whether it is a defective product or a mistake was made—wouldn't you want to know? A tough client will always point something out and it's up to you as the owner to find a way to improve your service or product. Perhaps the products you were selling came from a supplier who substituted your normal products with substandard ones and you didn't know. How else will you catch something or improve upon something if someone does not tell you?

Tough clients can be a blessing because they can show you what your company needs to work on. This can be difficult to take but attempt to see past their frustrations and hear what they need. They are providing you with information that can either make them a loyal client or inform new ways you can improve on your current service or product. However, if you are unable to meet their needs, then be honest. Honesty goes a long way and perhaps the tough client will become easier once they understand your limitations, or perhaps you can help them find someone else to serve them.

Let's say both the good client and the tough client ask you for help. Who are you going to assist? Is your choice fair? Who will more likely come back or recommend your services? I can say from experience that when you go out of your way to support the needs of a client—even if it means sending them to your competition—they will remember you went out of your way. They will respect you for your honesty and recommend others to your company who may be more suitable.

Shopping For Us, Not You

This next experience is a good example of what *not* to do. A few years back, my daughter and I went shopping for her graduation dress. We went into this lovely shop and started browsing. A saleslady—we realized later she was also the owner—came up and asked what we were looking for, starting the usual conversation about dress shopping. She picked out a few dresses for my daughter to try, dresses which my daughter was not overly interested but she tried one on as suggested. As soon as my daughter put on the dress, the sales lady kept saying we should purchase it.

Even when it was clear that my daughter was not at all happy with the dress, the owner continued to try talking us into buying it. We started to look at another dress, which is when the saleslady started bashing her competition across the street. She went on and on, seeming to forget that we were there to dress shop for my daughter, not to listen to her complaints about another business

My daughter and I both could not get out of that shop fast enough! The negativity and lack of customer focus definitely turned us off of spending any money or time in her store. Although we were polite and did not respond to her comments, we have no desire to return.

We all have issues, frustrations, and struggles in business. However, potential clients are not there to serve your problems, they are looking to you to solve theirs. Take the time to look after the people who support your business and listen to what they need.

2.10 Competition

Pay attention to changes, innovate your business,
innovate your skills and yourself.
Make your company a valued commodity.

Competition is an important part of business. Do you wonder why? Isn't it better not having competition and instead, monopolize the market? Let's look at the benefits of competition.

When there are competing businesses, customers get the best possible prices, quantity and even the quality of goods and services are affected. How do the businesses benefit?

I really like *Forbes* magazine as a business resource. One article called, "Five Reasons Why Competition Is Good For Your Business"[22] speaks about how business owners come up with better ideas because there is competition. If you do not have competition, it is difficult to have the motivation to improve, find another way to address a problem or search out a new resource.

If your business and your competitors are all doing the same thing, it becomes hard to distinguish your company from others. If you have something unique about your business, you will be attracting a market that perhaps your competition is not targeting, even though you provide the same services or products.

Lending A Hand, Lending A Truck

Here is another example of competition supporting the entire industry. I was working with a trucking company and our key competitor ran into a problem with a broken-down truck. This put the competitor in a difficult position to address their client's

---

[22] Five Reasons Why Competition Is Good For Your Business.
https://www.forbes.com/pictures/emjl45fhdh/understanding-your-core-market/#1c4d0b11d37f

needs. So we sent out one of our trucks to complete the job for them. Not only did our company help out the competition, we didn't charge our competitor for this one-time service. We even sent a detailed invoice with a $0.00 balance owing stating "business courtesy".

Not only was the competitor floored with our response, they were grateful for the hand. Bottomline, you will never make everyone happy and having a competitor is healthy. It's important to treat one another with respect as there will be days you will need each other in order to meet your own or a client's needs. When you make customers the most important, they really notice and will recommend you both.

This is a good reminder that specializing and/or offering a slightly different type of service from your competitor is complementary and beneficial to both, rather than something negative. Something to think about.

The Hotel Next Door

My girlfriends and I booked a Fall trip to Whistler for a race in which we were all taking part as team. My friend, Natalie, had organized the accommodations in a hotel near the starting line. When we arrived, the hotel was in the middle of renovations that were far behind their estimated timetable so they were unable to accommodate us. This was somewhat infuriating as all the hotels in the area were booked and we had paid a deposit a month prior. The hotel manager intervened and quickly made a phone call to the resort next door, securing accommodations for us right away and at the same price we were quoted originally.

Imagined our surprise when we ended up in a beautiful, two-bedroom unit right on the race course. We got to have coffee in the morning while the first groups were running the course and we got to cheer on the participants from our deck while we were having breakfast! It was a perfect spot and absolutely memorable.

When we checked out several days later, we asked if we could book the same room the following month. It turns out the cost was four times what we paid that weekend! We were quite taken aback—the hotel we had initially booked had paid the difference for us to stay in their competitor's hotel.

The result was four, happy women who thoroughly enjoyed their trip and were very grateful to the hotel for solving a customer problem in such a generous way. I would suggest both hotels to travelers.

Competition improves customer service. To compete, you cannot be complacent. Any company that is complacent will become extinct! By consistently encouraging your staff to innovate and improve their skills and services, you will maintain your loyal customers *and* attract a new customer base.

Defining Your Target Market

Competition forces you to focus on your "target market". Who is your target market? Have you clearly defined them?

Suzanne Doyle-Ingram holds training sessions to help her clients reach their goals, and one of the key aspects in her training is she asks each of her participants to clearly identify their target market. "Really drill down to the details as to who this person is and even give him or her a name, describe their lifestyle and their habits." This is such a valuable tool. Have you done this?

We all want to say that anyone can use our product or service but the reality is, it is a very specific market that is purchasing your services and products. Take your current clientele list and identify the following:

- Their average age?
- What is their gender?
- Do they have families?
- What hobbies or activities do they have?

- What shopping areas do they frequent?
- What are their needs?
- What information are they seeking?
- What is their economic status?

Look for commonalities among your clients. You may surprise yourself with the results.

By identifying your customers, you are better armed to provide for that person or group and create a marketing plan around your target market. Consider offering something a little different from everyone else in your industry. Stand out and celebrate your differences.

3. SAVING MONEY - PLUGGING THE LEAKS

"Make sure everyone is rowing the boat and not drilling holes when you are not looking." - <u>Steve Maraboli</u>,[23]

It's a hot summer day. You and the kids are looking for ways to stay cool so you go to your local store and find an affordable inflatable pool. Yes! This is the one! Cheap, easy to set up and *voila*, your kids are playing in the pool while you sit with your feet in sipping wine. Ahh, the life!

Later that night, the local racoons, also looking for ways to stay cool, stop in to take a dip, drink the water or perhaps wash their newly-found fruit in your lovely, inflatable pool. Imagine how disappointed the children (and you) will be the next day to find the pool totally deflated on the grass, mud puddles pooling with leaked water.

In this case, the racoons were the culprits, but there are so many other potential causes for damage to the inflatable pool— other animals, the children's water toys, or general horse play around the pool. There are a lot of things beyond your control that could cause the damage.

Perhaps you should have purchased the pool with the hard walls? Or perhaps an inground pool would be better? In any case,

---

[23] Stevemaraboli - https://stevemaraboli.tumblr.com/post/118386884225/know-your-circle-make-sure-everybody-in-your

without regular maintenance on your pool or some sort of controls regarding activities in and around it, your pool is bound to leak or have issues.

Just like with a pool, there are things which you can and cannot control in business, things you cannot even imagine happening. Then there are the costs involved in protecting and maintaining your business. The difference between a business that succeeds and one that fails is usually due to a number of common errors. We have already mentioned a few in previous chapters—cash flow management, customer service, and internal systems. Now we will focus on "saving money" and I will introduce a number of strategies you can use in the next few chapters.

3.1 Does Cash in the Bank Mean You're Making a Profit?

Items may appear bigger than reality.

A common mistake made by business owners is equating a positive bank balance with having profit. Cash flowing in and out of your bank account and a positive balance are positive signs but do not provide a complete picture of how well your business is doing. "Whohoo, I have $60,000 in the bank!" They think they are doing well. It makes me cringe when business owners believe their positive bank balance means they are fine.

Yes, a positive bank balance is a good sign that you are maintaining a bank balance, that you "may" not be operating in the red. However this is what I see: the outstanding payables balance, the level of payroll needed to maintain for a period of 3 to 6 months, how long can a company last if there is a seasonal slowdown or the company needs to replace needed equipment, or if the owner falls ill.

The first question you need ask and answer is: "How much do I owe right now? In order to answer that question, do you have to go through a pile of invoices in your drawer that are outstanding to add them all up?

What about sales taxes? Payroll remittances? Or a better question, how much do you owe for payroll and what if you had to close the doors, how much do you need to pay your employees the required payouts?

It is surprising that many business owners cannot answer these questions with any real accuracy. Some may have a good estimate based on the jobs they work or manage more closely, however, all the details like sales taxes, personal taxes, unexpected charges, interest, or numerous cash receipts are likely unknown without some digging.

When does the average business owner truly know the answer to these questions or know how much money they have actually made? Usually once a year at year-end, once all the accounts are updated and the accountant provides a bill for their services and another bill for the personal taxes owed, along with the financial statements.

This is a sobering annual event when the business owner will sit with their bookkeeper or accountant to have a conversation about the true state of their business. Perhaps the at this time, the business owner realizes the real potential of their bank account and that it does not have the funds to cover expenses.

If you are relying on a number on your bank statement, you are likely way off the mark by tens of thousands or even hundreds of thousands, depending on the amount of flow through in your business. Your bank balance may look good but consider the $40,000 worth of bills on the desk, and the payroll liability of another $15,000 is possibly not even included in your numbers! How about the many little cash receipts rolled up in a person's pocket, waiting to go through the wash, if they haven't already.

How many of you had the nice surprise of having lots of money left over? I can say by experience, not very many. Mind you, if you are hugely successful, it does happen.

What does it matter if you are not aware of what you owe? Does it really have an impact on your business? Well, if you can stay on top of the monthly bills and you are happy with status quo, then, like many proprietors, a once-a-year meeting may be all you need. However, if you need a loan for broken-down equipment, want to expand your business, need to apply for a mortgage or take part in another enterprising opportunity, more frequent check-ins are necessary.

Like many business owners, you want to minimize your tax liability or paying a $20,000 annual personal tax bill. So, you claim everything you can and do not pay yourself a proper wage. However, all of a sudden, the following happens:

- You cannot qualify for a mortgage.
- You cannot claim as much in CPP (Canadian Pension Plan is partially based on what a person earns or claims).
- You cannot get a business loan to cover new or replacement equipment.

Employees have deductions taken directly from their paycheques each time they are paid so their tax bill at year end will be relatively low. Whereas business owners often avoid paying their quarterly installments and end up with an ugly bill from the government based upon their earnings, now owing tens of thousands of dollars. bills can be painful if they are not planned for.

This is often when I get a call from a panicked entrepreneur, "How can this be?! What happened?!" Whether it is personal taxes or sales taxes, these huge bills can be devasting for a small business owner if they did not plan for it or set aside funds.

Maybe this has happened to you and you struggled through the payments. Now you are wondering what you can do to avoid a recurrence.

Many entrepreneurs may be great at making money, however, in my experience, over 80% of entrepreneurs have no idea about their required filings and the importance of staying on top of their government paperwork. They may have local, federal or industry requirements that need systematic attention.

Hopefully this is not you, but often, many entrepreneurs do end up with a large amount owing at the end of the year. Think about it this way: as an employee, you have money withheld from your paycheque each pay period for taxes, benefits, etc. The approximate taxes are submitted to the government on your behalf, so your end-of-year tax bill is either greatly reduced or you get a refund. Basically, you are prepaying your taxes so that you aren't surprised or unprepared at the end of the year.

This is the painless way of taking care of your personal tax bill. However, as a business owner, you are responsible for paying both the employee and employer portion of your taxes.

One of the main tax rules I have for my clients is to set aside money each month specifically for their taxes. I suggest about 20% of net income. The calculation is:

Gross Sales – Business Expenses = Net Income
NET Income x 20% = money to be set aside for taxes
(consider paying in quarterly installments)

Net income is what establishes your tax rate.

Every new business owner asks me to write off everything I can so they pay as little tax as possible. You certainly should not pay more than what's required for your taxes, yet entrepreneurs do not realize how this is a double-edged sword. What is often forgotten is that if you are not paying taxes, then you are not making money! Let's say, for many years, legitimate expenses keep your business' taxable income low, low enough to avoid taxes or a relatively small amount like $3,000 a year. If you then choose to apply for a mortgage or a loan for new business equipment, guess what? The banks will say, "You do not qualify."

By claiming all of your income and aiming for a healthy profit, and yes, paying taxes on that income generated, only then will you be able to qualify for loans and mortgages.

Regularly filing taxes and tax remittances will always limit a huge bill at the end of the year and most importantly, it forces your business to stay on top of the books. This becomes a blessing in disguise: staying on top of all your day-to-day income and expense tracking provides the opportunity for making key decisions easier when they come along. Remember, if you are paying taxes, it is a sign that you are making money. Plan for income and plan to pay your taxes on a regular basis.

3.2 Do This if You Wish to be Audited

"You always think you want to be noticed. Until you are."
—Sarah Dessen[24]

If you want the attention of the government, just avoid reporting your required filings and remittances, or do just like Shirley below—she certainly got their attention! I know you chose this book to find money-saving tips, well, in this chapter we will discuss the most common issues and costly mistakes businesses make every year.

Shirley runs her own hair salon and was getting by month to month—paying for staff, overhead for the building, supplies and other general business expenses. One day, Shirley calls me in an absolute panic, "My bank accounts are frozen!"

I go to her office and ask what happened. I had indeed filed her taxes; I would come in and file her sales taxes quarterly, but I quickly discovered the problem. Shirley had not paid the amounts owing. To make matters worse, Shirley has numerous brown envelopes from the government sitting on her desk, unopened. These envelopes contain the explanation for her dilemma. The government was demanding payment for the amounts owed, along with requests, warnings, 1st, 2nd and final warnings to address the amounts or further steps would ensue.

Once the government steps in like this, no accountant or book-keeper can help you. The government will speak only with you, the owner, as you are the only one with the authority to make payment arrangements at this point. They will only release your bank accounts once the amounts owed are paid, along with the interest and penalty fees.

---

[24] https://www.goodreads.com/work/quotes/42576172-saint-anything

Even if there is adequate money in the bank to pay your amount, the process of releasing your accounts can be long. This may mean you have to borrow funds to pay your tax bill while you wait for the government to release your account, and that is even if you qualify.

Please understand, when your bank account is frozen, you cannot cash business cheques, you cannot deposit money into the account, you cannot pay your employees out of the account, and your suppliers cannot cash your cheques. Even credit card payments that are deposited into your account will be held with the company that is supposed to deposit the money until the bank account is released. Basically, you will be unable to pay bills, nor can you receive funds or make any deposits to your account. This includes credit card deposits through your POS machine.

Shirley should have opened or given me the numerous warnings and letters to pay the amounts. If I had known about the amount owing, as her bookkeeper I would have informed her of the proceedings! This process takes time, and a business owner will receive a lot of notice before the government interferes with your bank account. Do not ignore notices from the government!

If you want the attention of the government, just avoid reporting your required filings and remittances and ignore their notices. Just like Shirley, she certainly got their attention! I know you chose this book to find money saving tips, well here is one of the most common issues with business every year and also, one of the more costly mistakes made.

Let's test your knowledge: Do you know when you need to remit government remittances? Reports like payroll remittances, sales tax reports and or Workers Compensation reports? Now here is the real question, are you aware of how much it can cost you and your business if you do not file these on time?

If you fail to file your taxes after three or more years, the government can assess you an outrageous amount to pay (note, the amounts determined by the government are calculations which are often not shared with us). If you do not file and/or fight it within a specified time frame, you will be on the hook for the expense and there is nothing anyone can do to help you. This will now be your amount owed to the government.

Most small business owners either do not know when they are to remit their reports or they submit or pay their remittances late. This is one, sure-fire way of getting chosen for, wait for it, an AUDIT! Yes, you, too, get the full attention of the government, all because of your delinquency with any government-required filing and/or payments owed.

Everyone gets busy as a business owner or manager; you have a lot on your mind, employee matters, missing purchases, deadlines, the list is an overwhelming one! Each day, you need to make hundreds of decisions in a short time frame and some take more time to sift and sort through. However, looming deadlines for filing government reports should be a priority. It amazes me when I get a phone call from a business owner asking me for help when they are honoured with an audit.

If the gentle reminders requesting you file don't work, the government will personally visit you at your place of business. Of course, you will be notified of their intention to visit in advance so that you can ensure everything they requested to review is prepared for their visit. Yes, they will send you a detailed list of the items you may need to provide. Then of course, they will assess whether the fee and penalties imposed for not filing are appropriate.

I had one client named Tony that operates a small landscaping company. Apparently, the government finally got his attention and slammed him with penalties for not filing his personal income taxes—he ran a business as a proprietor and had not filed his taxes for eight years. Tony hoped I could help him out so I sent him on a task to gather up all of the receipts and bank statements he could locate so that I could figure out his earnings and potential expenses. Fortunately, his business was not complicated, and he only had a few regular clients and relatively few one-time clients.

I went through all his information and receipts and completed eight years' worth of taxes. The result was very frustrating for Tony. If he had filed his taxes each year, he would have gotten a refund for most of the years I filed for him. Unfortunately, due to the number of tax years outstanding, the penalties charged for not filing and the interest on the penalties negated any refund he would have received. Plus, he still owed another $21,000!

The fees for not filing at the required deadlines can be substantial, and, if as a business owner you fail to set aside funds, you could find yourself in a cash flow crunch that can either put you out of business or require a second mortgage to pay the balance owed. At the very least, this could create an unnecessary strain on your ability to make decisions.

Other concerns of Liability

What most business owners do not understand is, payroll deductions and sales taxes are considered "trust money." What does that mean to you? It means you have collected money on another's behalf and, here is the kicker, it does not belong to you or your business.

You are required to submit the trust monies to the appropriate government authority either monthly, quarterly or annually. If you do not, they can hold you personally liable for these funds. If you are a board member of a non-profit, you can and will be held liable for any trust funds not paid to the government. It is in yours and your family's best interest to ensure this is paid.

Payroll remittances are the monies held back off an employee's cheque to put towards taxes. This is considered 'trust money' as it does not belong to the owner, or the employee as it was withheld on the behalf of the employee and due and payable to the government directly. Anything that is considered 'trust money', the government can and will hold you personally liable for those funds, not something to mess with.

I know of a young couple who runs their own business. They have over five staff and struggle along running their business month to month. Like Shirley, they also had their bank account frozen due to a similar situation as they were not reporting their payroll remittances nor were, they are submitting these funds to the government. Although they were not my clients, their mother, a dear friend of mine, shared her frustration to me. In this case, the couple had not filed and paid their taxes or payroll remittances for a few years.

Because the young couple's funds were frozen, they had no way to pay their employees. In this case, they were lucky to have a family member with funds and credit cards to carry them over nine months in cash flow until the account was released. This young couple had to borrow over $90,000 from family to make payroll each month, just to keep their business going until it was settled.

Without the help of their family member, not only were they unable to make payroll to keep their company running, this also meant they were unable to feed their family. In this case, family was key in helping the young couple through this difficult time. They have since filed everything regularly and are keeping up with regular payments for all the government taxes and remittances.

Events like these are often the "catalyst" for motivating a business owner to ensure they have or are meeting expectations. Note, these are costly learning curves which can ruin your business, your reputation, and the reputation of your business in your community.

And don't forget all the extra unnecessary costs in fees and penalties (in some cases).

Keys to remember:

- Stay on top of your required filing.
- If you have a payment schedule with the government, make sure you follow through with any agreement you make with them.

- For goodness sakes, open and read all the correspondence from the government!

By understanding the importance of doing and maintaining your books for your company and setting money aside to address tax bills, this will enable a business owner to make key decisions at the most important times.

3.3 Payment Methods and Protecting Your Cash

Take stock in what is going on and to be
aware of key indicators of a potential problem.

Let's talk about payment methods. All have pros and cons to them and with the many changes to our current banking system, it is important to use the best tools.

Cheques

Yes, people still use this method and it works fine except for a few glitches. The first issue, due to our banking system automation, is that cheques are not thoroughly reviewed, thus, the onus falls upon the business owner to verify the legitimacy of cheques being processed.

One of the managers I worked with in a large firm would pop into head office once a week for meetings. Of course, he, Banner, would routinely come into the payroll office, often seeking clarification on staff hours and benefits for his staff. On one of his visits to the office, Banner observed a stack of blank cheques sitting by the printer. This really bothered him so he spoke to the chief financial officer (CFO), Gary, to state his concerns about the cheques left out in the open. Gary did not seem bothered by this and felt that with the current processes, there was no need for locking up the cheques, due to limited access to the main office. However, the staff in the payroll office would frequently have meetings in another room, or be in the lunchroom for coffee or snacks, effectively leaving the office wide open to others in the office—staff or visitors.

Banner was quite upset that his concerns were not taken seriously so he walked into the payroll office, took a cheque, went back into Gary's office and in front of Gary wrote and signed a cheque in the amount of $20,000!

Now, this organization required two different approved signatories to sign the cheques. Banner was not one them. Gary just laughed and stated, "That will never go through."

Banner just smiled and said, "I hope not, but I can almost guarantee it will."

A week later, Banner walked into the office with a personal cheque from his own account for the $20,000 amount he had written to himself on the company cheque. Gary was astonished that the cheque was successfully cashed with no questions asked.

Due to good ol' automation, no one personally verified the legitimacy of the cheque. The banks only look at the electronic bank code at the bottom of the cheque and the amount. Basically, I can take anyone's cheque book, write a cheque to myself, sign it and it would go through. If that is not scary, I do not know what is.

In another situation, Gloria, one of our contractors, would bill us monthly and we would send her cheques each month. Pretty routine except that one month, Gloria contacted the office to ask when to expect her October payment. I thought it was odd because I knew it had sent and when I reviewed the bank statements, her October cheque had indeed cleared the bank. I figured she had just forgotten and misapplied the payment. So, I sent her the backup, the copy of the front and back of the cheque.

That's when Gloria got back to me stating that it was not her signature on the back of the cheque and she never received the deposit in her bank account.

I went back to previous payments made to Gloria and was able to compare the signatures on the back of the cheques from prior payments made to her. She was right! The signature and the bank information that was stamped on the bank was different from all other payments made. We went to the bank for an explanation as it clearly did not go to the intended recipient.

The bank was able to identify that it was not Gloria that had received the payment, but an Interac® machine deposit to another account holder. Although the bank had this information, they refused to do anything until Gloria filed an official complaint with the bank to address the misapplied payment. The sad thing was that Gloria's mail had been received by her neighbour in error. However, being so close to Christmas, the family was short, so they deposited Gloria's cheque into their own personal bank account via Interac® deposit.

This situation became very uncomfortable between Gloria and her neighbours. The worst part was, even though the bank recognized the error, they would not fix it or deal with the situation unless Gloria filed a complaint and a charge against her neighbour. Normally, one would think that the bank should take responsibility for allowing the deposit of Gloria's cheque into a different account with a different name. I thought that would have been a simple fix. Instead, it turned into an uncomfortable situation between neighbours.

Bottomline, you have 30 days from the time you receive your bank statement to dispute an error. After three months, the bank will likely not deal with any issues unless there are lawyers involved. Don't wait, verify the information on your statements. I cannot stress this enough.

Etransfers

Etransfers are another option. These are great, as they will go to the intended recipient and the transaction is password protected. Only the sender and recipient should know the password.

The other positive, you can only send funds that are available in your bank account. Unlike post-dated cheques, when the other company gets around to depositing your payment, weeks may have passed. Due to the changing levels of cash flow in your bank account, the cheque cashing could hit your account at an inopportune time, potentially causing the check to be returned and non-sufficient funds (NSF) fees applied. NSF fees used to be relatively cheap, but these days, a $45.00 fee on one returned payment is significant, especially with limited funds in your account.

Unfortunately, many small businesses running so close to the negative line often rack up a lot of unnecessary extra bank charges. They do not closely monitor their dated transaction or ensure funds are available in their account to cover the anticipated expenses when withdrawal is due to occur. Unfortunately, I have seen hundreds of dollars each month in unnecessary extra bank fees, NSF fees and interest charges which will drag down a company.

PayPal®

PayPal® is a great service and more popular in the United States than in Canada. However, be aware of scams surrounding PayPal in which the person states they have not received the product, so PayPal® returns the customer's money. Now you are out a product and the money, including any processing fees.

Credit Cards

Credit card payments are great, too, but with any online shopping, your credit card information can be put at risk. Always try to have one specific credit card with a limited value for online purchases to avoid incurring potential losses. Credit card companies are mostly diligent in offering some fraud protection to their card holders and are quick to alert you of activity that is out of the ordinary.

Telpay and Square are other great options. Offering a variety of safe payment options for your customers and suppliers makes payments easier and limits your liability should something go awry. Having a few payment options is helpful in making payments to your staff, contractors, or suppliers in a timely fashion and limits potential unnecessary losses to your company.

3.4 Are You Reviewing Your Bills?

One of the best ways to save money is not to spend it.

A common financial philosophy is that one of the best ways to save money is not to spend it. I recently had my summer tires replaced with my winter ones. The rims for my winter tires were already attached. I phoned my mechanic earlier in the day to verify the costs and I was told that because my tires and rims were already together, the cost was $45 plus taxes. After the switch was complete, I went to pay my bill and it was $54. I realize taxes are a part of the expense, however, this was more than the PST and GST normally charged.

Of course, I asked what the extra charges were as I was quoted only $45. They reviewed and found they had tacked on a "shop supplies charge". There was no requirement for extra supplies for such a job unless it was to fix a tire, which, of course was not the case. The "shop supplies charge" was another $4.00 with taxes, so the charges increased my bill from the expected amount to an extra $4.50 for no reason!

Seems like a minor extra expense that is often overlooked and would not have been questioned. However, let's consider 10 clients a day charged an extra $4.00. The company receives an extra $40 or $400 per month for nothing. Not even the cashier would be wiser to this unless it was pointed out to them by a diligent, eagle-eye customer reviewing their bills and expenses.

Other bills we pay each month that sometimes have extra charges are our phone, internet and cable bills. These services are known to add a random $5 charge. Sometimes these charges are from another source, however, if you pay the extra charges you are stating you are in agreement with the extra charge. Think about it, a $90 monthly bill with an extra $5 charge is easy to overlook. Sometimes it is billed every time, sometimes it is a one-off.

Cable companies will randomly provide extra channels for free for a few months and if you do not notice or do not cancel these extra channels after the promotional period, you are billed for those extra channels on an ongoing basis. It is very likely that these extra services were not requested and perhaps you were not even aware of the promotion. Wham! A hefty new extra charge on your bill. Even if you did not request these channels, you are now paying for them. Although this does not seem right or legal, it is common practice. Just like the company adding the extra $4 charge unexpectedly, cable companies can capitalize on your lack of attention to your bills!

You are probably thinking, "How is this allowed? How is this legal? What can we do about this?"

The answer to your questions is "buyer beware". The onus is on the customer to verify that charges are indeed correct.

These days, bills are online and when you click to view your bill, what you see may be a summary. In order to view a detailed bill, you may need to open a link under each category or click elsewhere or download a pdf. This may feel like a time-consuming task so many people skip it. They just want to get their bill paid, but, *voila,* unexpected charges have been paid and the company just made extra money off you.

Often, business owners are busy and only glance at their bills. They see a bill that needs attention and they just pay from their banking app so they can take care of it right away.

So, what do you need to look for in a bill? Here is a checklist:

- Your business name or intermediary's name. This clearly identifies who has to pay. Often, a business will issue an invoice with a name on it, however, if they are not incorpo-rated, you may need to pay the owner of the business in their name.

- Are the expenses listed for agreed-upon prices for the agreed-upon goods and services? Are there extra costs such as an administrative fee or a processing fee (which should not be on the bill)? Is there a fee for miscellaneous parts or an inapplicable freight charge?

- Are there taxes added to the bill? If so, their tax number should be listed on the invoice so that you can verify if it is legitimate. Any bill over $30 in value should show their tax registrant number for the sales taxes being charged. (For a Canadian invoice of $100 or more that shows sales taxes being charged, the invoice should include the company's GST number.)

- Is there a date on the bill that clearly identifies when the items were shipped or billed for? I have received invoices from one company from three years prior! To not bill for such a long time is hardly acceptable for any business. Chances are, they may not ever get paid.

- What is the currency on the invoice? USD? CAD? EUR? What currency should payment be sent? Was this agreed upon at the time of purchase?

- What is the Total Amount Due? The amount due must be listed on the bill along with any specific payment terms. Examples of payment terms found on bills:

o Pay within 15 days, apply a 2% discount on the bill.
o Due and payable within 30 days.
o Any amount unpaid after 30 days will be charged interest on the balance owing equal to 1.5% per month.

o   Due within 10 days.

Most bills from the same supplier are standard and expected, however, small changes or small, unapproved expenses might pop up and if you pay them, then recourse is limited. Note: errors do happen so ask for clarification about extra charges. Avoid placing blame, just be prudent in your review of your bills. Knowing why or for what you are being charged is practicing thoroughness and discipline in managing your business' expenses.

Beware of Scams

There is a new email scam going around recently. It targets companies that list the names of their key staff and managers on their website. The scammers will create an email address with a staff's name on it. Then they will contact a different staff member, usually the finance person, and ask for a financial process to happen quickly, asap. Now, when a person receives a request from their boss, of course they will start the process as requested. I almost got caught up in this very scam.

This scammer had contacted the office to speak with our boss and when he answered, the scammer would hang up. However, when the scammer was told that the boss was in a meeting, the request would suddenly appear in my email. The request was for less than $10,000 and I would ask for details. The scammer would respond with an address and another email to put a rush on the request.

Of course, the request was an odd one, so I contacted my boss who was still in a meeting. I sent a text, to which he replied in large text, "What is this about?" He was not aware of any request. We put a hold on the payment, I went back to the email and yes, the email address was not my boss' at all. Initially I had assumed that our boss was working from home, a common occurrence, and

I assumed that the email he was using was coming from his personal email address.

This company has since implemented a rule to speak directly to one another prior to preparing any payment and not to prepare any payment requests via email or text. Yes, these scams are happening via text as well because many company websites post their staff's phone contact information.

This scam was reported immediately, especially since they provided an address to send payment, so this gave the police a way to follow up. There are several ways to report scams like this, please go to the section in the back of this book that lists websites explaining the most common scams and how/where to report them.

Quote vs. Invoice

Another common error happens because the difference between a quote and invoices is not made clear. Are you paying for an invoice? Or is it a work order or quote? You're probably thinking," What does it matter? If I hired the person to do the work, does it need to be an invoice upon completion of the job or transaction?"

A quote is often a number based upon a specific task or purchase for supplies. This number will usually state that taxes are not included in the number. Only on a final invoice would taxes be added. Also, quotes and work orders are often based on guesstimates, which may be different once the service is completed or the product is actually sent.

An invoice should clearly identify all the real-time costs involved, any extra costs for extra supplies, extra labour and if there are shipping charges. The taxes will then be included. An invoice should identify the work done and should compare correctly against the "approved list" or quote unless something happened. Sometimes, they were unable to do the work and you hired someone else. In this case, both a work order with one company and an invoice from another are paid.

Also, the invoice may show that the job took less time to complete and your invoice may be substantially less! I would hate to see anyone paying extra for something they did not need. It does happen.

One of my clients, George, instructed me to pay for a quote one time, so I prepared the payment and suggested he waited for the actual invoice and not pay the quote. He was in a rush, did not wish to bother with the details and asked me to send it out.

Within a few days, we received the actual invoice which was over $2,000 less than the quoted amount because the company was unable to do all the work asked of them. Therefore, they provided a discounted invoice. I managed to get a hold of the company and put a stop payment on the cheque and reissued another. George was very happy I had taken those steps and has since always ensures an invoice is submitted.

In another situation within a large company, the accountants approved a payment on a work order which was submitted late. The amount seemed familiar as they were a regular contractor that did several regular monthly tasks for the company. So before submitting payment, I went through all the company's prior payments and found that the contractor had already been paid for the work on the work order in front of me. This work order was for $80,000 and had been approved for payment by several people, until I was able to show that payment had already happened. Interestingly, upon doing the research, there were similar duplicate payments found with the same error and the company receiving the payments did not notify us.

Work orders are meant as a means of updating or tracking the work completed on a job. When the invoice comes in (which often looks very similar), work orders should be attached to the invoice to verify the work done. This practice could have helped us avoid the multiple payments above.

As well, watch for duplicate payments, as a work order number is different than the invoice number. This can be easily missed and only the company that receives the extra payment is the wiser.

Caveat emptor or buyer beware. It's all in the details and daily monitoring.

Tips for Reviewing Incoming Invoices

1. **Review your bills as they come in.** Set time aside each morning to deal with mail, approve the ones you want paid, and highlight the areas you want to question on bills for which you require more information.

2. **Get a detailed invoice.** Know what you are paying for and make sure the products and services listed are indeed what was agreed upon.

3. **Verify all the costs listed.** Are the costs listed according to what was agreed upon? Do they match the quote? Is there an explanation for the differences? Are there costs listed on the invoice that were not part of the job?

4. **Ensure that the work completed was indeed requested**. Have the person requesting this sign off on it (an initial on the invoice before paying is appropriate). This is important in larger companies; for a smaller business with limited decision makers, it is a straightforward process and an initial is not necessary as they are usually the ones who ordered and are paying for the expense.

Be aware of other types of documents that are not an invoice:

An estimate or a quote: Carries no obligation to pay as there is no agreement. It is an estimated amount based upon known factors, which the recipient may accept or reject.

A notice: Offering of an opportunity to receive a good or service at a specified rate and is an offer which the recipient may accept or reject. These are similar to unsolicited mail containing credit card offers. Again, no obligation to pay.

A packing slip: Is confirmation of items shipped, listing the quantity of the goods shipped. Presumably, there is some sort of agreement to pay for the goods shipped and should be matched up with the actual invoice which comes shortly thereafter.

Bills of lading: Are documents signed by a freight company or their agent to describe the freight and the consignee of the property.

The process of reviewing quotes and invoices in detail can be cumbersome and time-consuming for a larger corporation, but for a small business with limited decision makers, it is straightforward, relatively painless and an extremely important process.

3.5 Are You Paying for Illegitimate Sales Tax?

"You must pay taxes. But there's no law that says you gotta leave a tip."– Morgan Stanley[25]

When you receive an invoice, are you being charged GST, PST or sales taxes? Of course, for a Canadian company billing you GST and PST, it is highly likely that it is legitimate, however, before you pay the bill, have you confirmed that the company is actually a registrant of the sales taxes listed?

Here is a story I personally experienced. While I was working at a large firm in the accounts payables department, I received a bill to input that which was from a US company. The bill was in US dollars and it included GST and PST as charges in US currency. Approximately 98% of the time, the total bill would be paid as stated on it. Now, as a business owner, the invoice looked legitimate and similar to the many other invoices you see and go through, so why wouldn't this one be paid?

The question you need to ask: is their company registered as a GST and/or PST registrant? I researched this company and as it turned out, they certainly were not PST or a GST/HST registrant and should not be charging for the added expense. That is effectively a 12% bonus on their invoices!

Before you pay, review the following: with any invoice over the amount of $ 30.00,[26] the invoice must have the company's business number or GST number listed on the invoice if they have one. Note: some US businesses certainly do have a Canadian

[25] Morgan Stanley advertisement on Forbes website; https://www.forbes.com/pictures/fklf45kmm/morgan-stanley-advertisement/#55e603b21a94

[26] Canada Revenue Agency – https://www.canada.ca/content/dam/cra-arc/formspubs/pub/rc4022/rc4022-18e.pdf

presence and are a valid GST/HST registrant. Take the extra steps and verify.

If GST and/or PST are being charged on an invoice, they are required to list their sales tax numbers on the invoice. With this information and the company's legal name, you can verify if it is a legitimate tax number by going to the Canada Revenue Agency[27] and enter the following information:

- the company name.
- their 9-digit GST/HST number.

Note: if a business is operating as a proprietor (they are not a limited or corporate company), you will need the name of the owner to verify their GST status. To verify Sales Tax Licenses[28] for a company in the US, you have to dig a little more on their website as registrants are categorized by State.

Be aware that each state has very different rules and regulations in regards to their taxes.

---

[27]Canada Revenue Agency - https://www.canada.ca/en/revenue-agency/services/e-services/e-services-businesses/confirming-a-gst-hst-account-number/terms-conditions-use.html

[28]Salt Validators: Verify Sales and Use Tax, Resale, and Exemption Certificates https://validate.saltcert.com/

Be aware of the difference in currency and
how the actual value affects your real costs.

I recently experienced paying exorbitant charges due to currency differences! We were in Canada and looked up Canadian websites for hotels in which we could stay. We thought it was straightforward as we were on a Canadian website. We contacted one hotel to book a room for the night. We even called their local number in Vancouver!

We had a good night's sleep and proceeded on our trip the next day. A few days later, my girlfriend was reviewing her credit card charges and noticed that the agreed upon charge of $99 plus taxes ($110) was $145.25 in Canadian dollars! I understand that this may happen when travelling to different countries, however, we are within our own country in Canada, looking up Canadian websites. We were under the impression we were paying only $110CAD for the room, yet we ended up paying 31% more!

This is what happened: The hotel chain had another company take care of phone bookings. The difference between the US and CAD value was the company's fee for the five-minute booking call. Even though we were booking accommodation in the same country, we were being charged a US rate. This is infuriating to me, when a person is booking anything, the price's currency should be absolutely clear at the time of order. This is just another example about how different currencies are used to make more money and how important it is for us to have clarity on the fees being charged.

A similar circumstance concerns online travel planning. The prices clearly state that the rate is in Canadian dollars, yet, once you choose your flights and go to the payment page, the price automatically changes to US dollars. The amount quoted is the same, however, the company charges the amount as US dollars. This is the 30% increase in fees now unwittingly being charged to your credit card. Sneaky!

Try to get confirmation of prices in the appropriate currency and practice doing screen shots of what is quoted. This may provide you with some recourse when you dispute the bill. Be aware, there is often a catch or a box checked later on that may not allow for any type of recourse. It can be hard to fight but worth fighting for: 30% in extra unexpected charges can truly add up.

Not all credit cards offer the same benefits. Before, it was always a better idea to use your credit card to purchase items from outside of the country as the credit card company automatically makes the currency exchange. However, many credit cards are now charging a premium for this service, or a "foreign transaction fee", a fee of an extra 1.5– 3%. "This may not seem much at first, but at 2.5 % surcharge is 25.00 for every 1,000.00 spent!"[29]

There is also a dynamic currency conversion whereas the merchant may boast of no conversion fee yet downplay the fact that you will be charged an exorbitant exchange rate. It is the merchants who benefit from this added cost on your credit card! Merchants who offer this "dynamic currency conversion"[30] are required to give their customer the option to turn it down. Make sure they do, or you won't be able to dispute this charge.

I would strongly suggest that if you do a lot of out-of-country ordering with your credit card, that you shop around to see your options. Compare them, ask questions and read all the small print—the key is in the details.

---

[29]Million Dollar Journey https://milliondollarjourney.com/top-free-credit-cards-when-travelling-out-of-country.htm

[30] Foreign transaction vs. Currency Conversion Fees – Erin El Issa https://www.nerdwallet.com/blog/credit-cards/foreign-transaction-vs-currency-conversion-fees-difference/

I wish I could say which one is best, however all I can do is suggest you learn "how to Read a Schumer Box"[31] which is basically a cheat sheet for your credit card. It provides an at-a-glance reference on all the key fees to expect with that specific credit card. Another good resource is this recent post on *NerdWallet* of the "6 best no foreign transaction fee credit cards of January 2020"[32]

Currency differences are becoming a huge issue in our economy so be clear on how much you are paying for your product or service.

---

[31]How to Read a Schumer Box – Joseph Audette
https://www.nerdwallet.com/blog/credit-cards/how-to-read-schumer-box/

[32]6 Best No Foreign Transaction Fee Credit Cards of January 2020 – Robin Saks Frankel https://www.nerdwallet.com/best/credit-cards/no-foreign-transaction-fee

3.7 The Phobia of Brown Envelopes

When the government is ignored, it's like ignoring your mother,
the ramifications can and will be memorable, aka, harsh.

Remember Shirley, the salon owner from the previous auditing section? Remember the government notices she hadn't opened? There they were, ten unopened, brown envelopes. As I opened each enve-lope, one was a request for information, the next a demand to file, followed by the demand for a response within a timeframe and then another with a warning about freezing her accounts. There was all the information she needed, and the government's actions were clearly explainable.

General rule of thumb, the government will not take steps to freeze your accounts without lots of notice. Correspondence will state a timeframe before action is taken and they will clearly outline the steps a business owner needs to take to avert the freezing of their bank account. If Shirley had taken the time to open the envelopes, she could have averted three weeks of financial pain. To her surprise, there was absolutely nothing I could do as a bookkeeper, nor could an accountant or lawyer do anything on her behalf against the government. All I could do was hurry up and file all the required notices that needed filing. Just to be clear, none of the aforementioned professionals can speak on your behalf and until the government's demands are met; to unfreeze your bank accounts, you have to pay up.

Save yourself unnecessary pain and open the brown envelopes. Most times, it is just remittance statements for the next remitting period, however, the odd notice or request for information is just that, a request for information or a reassessment. All of these should be forwarded to your bookkeeper/accountant and all of them should be opened by you, the business owner. When you ignore requests, this inaction is a red flag to the government, alerting them of a potential issue for which they must take action.

Brown envelopes from the government do not contain a plague, they contain nuggets of information that the wise will open and review. If you receive a brown envelope, making a phone call to the government to clarify a letter of request will show good faith and that you are willing to work with them to address the issue. When the government is ignored, it's like ignoring your mother, the ramifications will be harsh.

Remember, the types of requests or information in the brown envelopes are remittances, requests to file, or just requests for supporting tax paperwork. If requests for paperwork are not sent within a certain timeframe, the government may just deny the credit or deduction. If you are requested to file something and this is ignored, the government assesses an amount using their calculations (which is a mystery at times) and if you do not file an objection within a certain time frame, you will be on the hook for it all. If you move, make sure that the government is notified (via tax filing) to ensure the letters get to you.

Another tip: Pay attention to brown envelopes with red ink on the outside. Red ink means you have been ignoring them, and this is like your mother's last warning before her wrath shows up.

3.8 Banking as a Small Business

"Wealth is not about having a lot of money;
it's about having a lot of options." – Chris Rock

Standards are always changing, and each bank or credit union has varying expectations or limits of tolerable debt levels which they are willing to fund.

What do financial institutions look for? Well, for smaller businesses, credit unions offer far more bang for your buck than a bank. This includes saving on regular bank fees and more tolerable levels of loan amounts. Non-profits in particular benefit more from working with a credit union.

Credit unions offer all the same services as a bank but can offer better rates for their local clients' business than a bank may. Banks have a very stringent mandate and as each year passes, the rules keep changing, making it harder for entrepreneurs to borrow funds.

Credit unions tend to better service the local businessperson and small businessperson due to cheaper fees yet have almost identical services as large banks. However, if you are a medium to large company which operates in more than one region, banks may be far easier to work with on an inter-provincial, national or international stage.

Banks and credit unions must follow the same laws, so often, the key to choosing your financial institution rests heavily upon the following factors:

- Accessibility.
- Relationship with an institution's representative.
- What the credit union or bank will do for you. (Credit unions will take more risk with a local business owner, where banks are far less flexible.)

- Who is willing to provide more business support (with loans, line of credit, online deposits)?

Just remember, banks and credit unions are businesses and must operate as such. They are not doing you a favour; they are providing a service. They exist to serve you the client, just like you and your business is serving your clients or customers. Do shop around, ask the same questions of each institution so you can compare.

As a bookkeeper, it makes my life and yours much easier if certain services are in place or offered:

- **Online banking.** This is imperative for you and your bookkeeper so you have the ability to see your statements in real time for reconciliation—ensuring you stay out of the red and for you to view and monitor the activities of your banking. There are ways to set up "view only" access.

- **Online payment of pre-approved bills**. The option to pay pre-approved bills online means your bookkeeper can handle this for you. Bills such as telephone services, govern-ment remittances (payroll & taxes), utilities companies, and other regular, monthly bills.

- **Direct deposit.** Ensure this is an option for yourself, your employees and your contractors, too. It's so handy and easy to set up! Once you have it for employees, it is not much more to add your key or regular contractors. Direct deposit as a payment option makes working with your company far more attractive.

- **Fee structures that match your level of business.** Some accounts offer lower fees if a specific amount is always kept in your account each month (e.g. $5,000).

- **A main representative.** Having a specific account manager as your main contact will help with sorting out any issues that arise. By building a relationship with your representative, you build a rapport, build trust, and importantly, a direct line to someone who can help you when there is a concern with your bank statements. Also, by building this relationship, there is an understanding of how you run your business and it may be easier to qualify for a much-needed loan for your business as banks do give credence to your credibility as a person.

- **Cheque deposit records show a cheque's front AND back.** Make sure your statements include a copy of the front AND back of cheques! There will likely be an extra fee for this but it's worth the money for identifying potential fraud.

So, what do financial institutions look for? The same things you look for on your financials, but also your ability to pay back a loan, the potential collateral you have—personally and business-wise—and of course, your credit.

3.9 Track Payment Deadlines and Avoid Unnecessary Fees

All strategies start with knowing what you need and when.

There are two aspects to this. Firstly, know what you need in the bank to cover expected expenses each week. A quick and easy way to determine this is to create a list of expected expenses and their due dates for payment. Use a calendar to remind yourself of the expected timelines for paying necessary expenses.

Tools of the Trade

Below is a simple example of one way to track expected expenses. As you can tell, it does not need to be difficult or techy, you can use something as simple as the calendar on your phone, or an actual printed calendar with notes listing the dates that payments are due, what they are for, and the expected amount of each.

Personally, I prefer to use my online calendar (Outlook[33] and Gmail[34] have them). The calendar can track meetings, payment dates, and deadlines, all colour coded. Plus, these tools provide reminders! As a bookkeeper, I rely heavily on these tools to ensure that specific payment deadlines are not missed and reports are provided on time.

Start by listing you company's expense deadlines such as: sales tax filing, tax filing, T4 filing dates, payroll and payroll remittances, loans and credit card payments. Write down or make an entry on your calendar. You can make this a recurring date

---

[33] How to create a recurring E-mail message in Outlook
https://docs.microsoft.com/en-us/outlook/troubleshoot/email-messages/create-recurring-email

[34]Create a recurring event
https://support.google.com/calendar/answer/37115?co=GENIE.Platform%3DDesktop&hl=en

(monthly, weekly, etc.). For each company I work with, I have pre-set these reminders for a year in advance!

Types of Expenses

There are three types of expenses: fixed, periodic and variable expenses.

Fixed expenses are items like salaries and wages, benefits payment due dates, telephone expenses, rent, hydro, loans and insur-ance. These are the regular, expected expenses where the amounts are relatively the same each month. These are due at the same time each month so start with these. On each date for each bill, write in how much is owed and for what.

Periodic expenses are those that are due and payable on a quarterly or semi-annual basis and are often forgotten about. These are items like quarterly sales tax remittances, WCB reporting or annual expenses like T4 remittances. For sales taxes, always estimate high-er in case sales increase so you are prepared for a specific amount.

Then there are the variable expenses. Variable expenses change, are infrequent, and often unexpected. Variable expenses are also considered discretionary or "unplanned" expenses. The unknown variables are why it is even more important to track expenses on a regular basis. Some of these unknown expenses can be either small amounts or extremely expensive, which can negatively affect your business. Don't get me wrong, we all have unplanned expenses come up, whether it is for new shoes, our daughter's dance recital, school trip, the need to hire and train someone, purchase new equipment, repairs to keep the equipment going, or perhaps there is a great sale that you can't pass up.

The good thing about variable expenses is that these can be controlled by behaviour, it's what we spend on food, clothing, coffee and treats. These expenses are controlled by our choices and desires, not necessarily by need. I may need a new computer, however, do I need the $2,400 computer or is the $600.00 computer sufficient? Yes, I am having a lunch meeting for the staff, so do we pay for individual meals or do we do buffet style?

Although variable expenses are the hardest to budget, these expenses are where you can exercise control. Remember how earlier in the book, we touched on living large too fast? Curtail your expenses and decipher between "need" and "want". The savings are largely in the variable expenses.

The best way to review how much in variable expenses you require each month is to review actual spending from the past three to four months of variable expenses. This will give you an approximate amount to set aside each month to cover the basic types of variable expenses.

Now that you have reminders set up, you should not be missing deadlines and incurring late fees and interest for late payments. That is, just as long as you do not ignore your reminders!

3.10 Procrastinating with Your Books

*"The true definition of procrastination is,
the art of screwing yourself." – Philips Benjamin*

For many, procrastination is the reason for so much more in our lives other than just staying on top of your books. For most business owners, it is due to the lack of time available to stay on top of their books or they do not possess the knowledge to do this themselves. For some, they just do not want to know how bad their situation really is. As they ignore the pile of paperwork sitting on the table, it becomes like an insurmountable task that they dread and put off until tax deadline draws near.

Not knowing where to start can be enough for anyone not to take action. And I can guarantee, "you will never be going to feel like it".[35] Do your children want to clean their rooms or help with the chores? Do you feel you have to motivate them with threats of losing privileges, desserts, etc.? I know it sure took a lot of energy out of me to motivate my children to help with the chores or do their homework. In fact, I have some great "crazy mom" stories that are really funny to share today. Bottomline, like our children, we will need to take the necessary steps to "force" ourselves to accomplish tasks which do not excite us. The key is simplifying the process.

It does not have to be hard and there are so many little steps—actionable steps—which you can do to make the pain of books and bookkeeping less daunting.

Let's start with the "why." Why is it important to stay on top of your books? Do you care? Why or how can it make a difference?

---

[35] Mel Robbins "How to Stop Screwing Yourself Over"
https://upliftconnect.com/how-to-stop-screwing-yourself-over/

Hopefully at this point in the book, you will understand the "why" or at least understand the importance of staying on top of your books.

In case you forgot, it's about saving money and making money so that you can be successful and live the life you choose, all the while, having happy customers.

One way is that as soon as you open the mail, you deal with it immediately. Sort the mail into bills to pay, invoices, and payments to deposit. Put any remittance forms or information you want your bookkeeper to deal with in another pile. Know that every time you pick up or open your email and don't deal with it, there could be several negative outcomes:

- You continue procrastinating.

- You waste time. (Each time you pick up or look at paperwork that you could deal with but don't, you could be using that time on other tasks.)

- You incur late fees.

One way to deal with your paperwork immediately is to use a receipt tracking app. As described previously, you take a picture with your phone and the file uploads into a cloud where your bookkeeper or accountant has access to the information.

A solutions-based bookkeeper or accountant will be able to identify areas requiring specific attention, areas that can make the gathering of information simpler, less taxing, and keeping the books up to date in a way that can free you up.

3.11 To be, or Not to be Audited

*Audit findings are easy to come across, it is the successful change
implemented from the findings which provides true value.*

Have you ever gone through an audit? They are time consuming
but very informative at the same time. The only reason for concern
in an audit is if you are unable to prove the income and expenses
that you are claiming.

What are some of the beneficial aspects of being audited?
Whether an audit is done internally or by outside sources like the
government, the purpose is to determine the adequacy of internal
controls, identify inefficiencies and waste, and ensure compliance
with regulations.

With industries that hold funds in trust, there are often
regulations that require them to have an outside source perform
the audit. When working with property management companies, I
would go through an annual audit as required by the laws
governing property management companies as they administer
"trust accounts".

I always found this process very informative and interesting as
auditors would always explain the changes in the laws and
provide tips on how to best meet the guidelines of the regulatory
bodies. It was a great learning opportunity as there is so much to
know and be aware of in each area that one needs to be a
specialist. The likelihood of the average business owner being
aware of the many guidelines may be small, but with
knowledgeable support of an experienced team (bookkeeper,
accountant) changes can be made in how best to address them.

Common Areas Where Auditors Find Errors

Mileage Rate per Kilometre

Each year, Revenue Canada provides a suggested prescribed rate for corporate mileage reimbursement. This is a rate that companies can provide to their staff as a benchmark for non-taxable reimbursement use of personal vehicles for business purposes. In one company I worked, a non-profit, the rate was $0.50 per kilometre. CRA's rate at that time was $0.54/km up to 5,000 km and only $0.48/km over and above the 5,000 km threshold.

The non-profit company did not adjust the mileage rate downwards to $0.48/km after the 5,000 km was exceeded, as they believed it was just easier to keep the rate the same across the board. That was, until I spoke with a senior accountant in an accounting firm. He quoted a recent court case in which another company was paying $0.04 less than the prescribed rate, therefore the government deemed the entire mileage reimbursement as taxable income in the hands of the employees!

I assumed that anything above the prescribed rates would be considered a taxable benefit, but under? Wow; based upon this court case, the allowable threshold is less than $0.04 either above or below the current CRA prescribed mileage rate. The following year, the CRA's rates increased to $0.59/km for the first 5,000 kilometres, and to $0.53/km for each additional kilometre."[36] These rates are posted by CRA annually. Wisely, the non-profit company adjusts their mileage rates to match CRA's prescribed rates each year.

Regardless of the mileage rate, the most common offense is in **_not having a mileage log._** It is a bit tedious of a task to constantly

[36] 2020 Automobile Deduction Limits https://www.canada.ca/en/department-finance/news/2019/12/government-announces-the-2020-automobile-deduction-limits-and-expense-benefit-rates-for-businesses.html

track the mileage for work purposes each day or each week, yet this is one area which most businesses do not take the time to track.

In one case, Liam, a realtor, would always tell me his approximate mileage at year end. As you can imagine, driving prospective buyers around all the time results in mileage that is quite high. On his 2015 tax return, Liam claimed 14,200 km resulting in a deduction of $7,668.00.

Liam was then chosen for an audit and was unable to provide the information to substantiate his claim. So, Liam had to wade through a year's work of his emails, calendars and day planners to be able to reconstruct a log. The newly-produced log was only able to substantiate approximately 9,600 km resulting in a deduction of $5,184.00. As a result, the additional tax ,plus penalties and interest, amounted to $857.43 for overclaiming mileage.

Mileage logs will save you a lot of headache, so remember, keep any calendars, day planners or any tracking you use with your related tax return for the same period, so you will always have the required information on hand.

Gift Cards & Gift Certificates

At Christmas time, it is common to offer gifts to your staff. Often a gift certificate or a gift card is provided as it is so much simpler of a gift when you are not sure what the recipient needs or likes. However, providing gift cards and gift certificates to your staff is "near cash" which is equivalent to receiving actual cash. Therefore, it is a taxable benefit to your employee/staff person, and you must include this in their income, applying payroll taxes off of the gift card's value.

[37] Gifts, Awards and Long-Service Awards https://www.canada.ca/en/revenue-agency/services/tax/businesses/topics/payroll/benefits-allowances/gifts-awards-social-events/gifts-awards-long-service-awards.html

"A near-cash item is one that functions as cash, such as a gift certificate or gift card, or an item that can be easily converted to cash, such as gold nuggets, securities, or stocks."[37]

If you wish to provide a non-cash gift to a staff member, it must be an item of which the total value, *including sales taxes*, does not exceed $500.00 in value. Any value above $500.00 is considered a taxable benefit and must be included in the employee's income. There are indeed other rules around this area, but an area that is an easy target in an audit. Ensure you have all the information when providing gifts to your staff.

Meals and Entertainment

This is an area where a business owner is considered as receiving a personal benefit (food), therefore, only half of the meal cost can be used on his business taxes. It is important to record the full amount in your company books; it is on the tax return that the 50% is applied.

Of important note, only half of the GST paid out on the meal should be recorded in your company's books. Only half of the expense is a business expense, therefore only half of the sales taxes should be taken as a sales tax credit.

Example: Total meal cost is; $21.22, GST is 1.06 plus tip 15% tip is $3.34 = total cost of meal is $25.59.

To record this entry, it will look like this:

	Debit	Credit
Meals & Entertainment	25.06	
GST (only 50% of GST)	0.53	
Bank (or how it was paid)		25.59
	25.59	25.59

When the taxes are filed, the full meal cost is entered and automatically adjusted on the taxes to record only ½ of the meal's expense. The GST input tax credit will have been applied correctly.

Another detail to note about meal deductions is having the receipt annotated with the following details:

- Description of the customer, client, or associate present at the meal or entertainment.
- Business purpose of the meal or entertainment.
- Profit Motive for providing the meal or entertainment.
- Proof of payment and who paid.

At the conclusion of a business meal, be diligent about writing who you're with, the business purpose, and profit motive.

Employer-Sponsored Events
Many businesses miss the benefit of claiming this or they just claim it under the wrong area. Here is an example:

Sheila always liked to treat her staff each year to a big Christmas dinner. She would also include the cost of the hotel overnight so that staff could relax and enjoy themselves. The rule to follow for this type of meal expense is ensuring that the cost of the event does not exceed $150.00 per person. You can then expense the full amount. This can be done 4 to 6 times a year.

Most bookkeepers would just put the expense under Meals and Entertainment. However, in doing that, they would effectively lose 50% of the expense when filing their taxes. So, enter the claim under "Advertising" as it is about boosting employee morale. This will ensure that the full expense can be claimed.

Please note, if the cost of the event exceeds $150.00 per person, then the company must claim this under Meals and Entertainment and only 50% of the expense can be claimed on the taxes.

Copies of credit card or bank statements do not suffice as proof.
This is a common misconception among business owners. Let's say Johnny goes to Canadian Tire to buy the tools he needs for his mechanic shop. He purchases a number of tools, but also other items that Canadian Tire also offers. Just a listing on a credit card statement is not enough to prove full work-related expense. One of those 900 receipts on the statement could have been for a trampoline for Johnny's children and not tools.

If you are audited by the GST/HST department, they will require the actual receipt clearly listing the sales taxes paid as it may have been a payment for a deposit, which does not have GST/HST. Or perhaps the receipt was actually for the trampoline and not tools, therefore the expense and the sales taxes are disallowed.

Life Insurance
The cost of personal life insurance is not a deductible business expense. Many business owners have their life insurance fees come out of the business account. I never claim it as an expense, I only put the expense towards the owner's equity account. There are some provisions if the insurance is on a loan for the business, however, look into the proper calculations for this.

Pros of an Audit
Often, the result of an audit was the ability to identify areas that required improvement, then we could and would implement the suggested changes. Ultimately, we would improve our understanding of our own working systems and we would have improved financial systems.

The expertise of an auditor is very useful because there is so much to know when it comes to expenses and claims. While working for the government, we had a GST audit. The auditor came in with three binders, all six inches thick, with all the rules and regulations, the exceptions, and the most recent changes. I had no idea there was so much to one sales tax!

Even though this auditor was seasoned, he would still need to flip back and forth through the binders to verify the rules and regulations for GST. In the government system, there are special rules around the percentages of the GST which can be claimed as an input tax credit and each department had its own special rules. The only way to know all the rules is to become an expert. Auditors are indeed experts in their respective areas and these specialist auditors can be helpful in ensuring you are operating under the right regulations. They may even provide information as to extra tax credits available if your industry falls under certain items. Call me crazy, but I have learned a lot through audits.

Employee vs Contactor

This is probably one of the biggest areas for an audit. I could write a book on the many individual cases and how each scenario plays out. If you have a person who regularly helps you in the course of running your business, are you treating them as a contractor and just paying them a flat rate per hour or are you treating them as an employee and withholding payroll taxes on their behalf and remitting them? If you are at all unsure as to whether or not the person should be an employee or a contractor, then I suggest you ask your accountant or bookkeeper for clarification in your specific case.

Dominique ran an office assistant business and had several people who would take on certain tasks on a regular basis. One of her workers, Cheryl, would come to her office, organize the files, answer the phone, cover for when Dominque was away, and carry out tasks as requested by Dominique.

The CRA came in to do an audit and realized that Dominique was paying Cheryl as a contractor, just paying her $15.00/hour. The CRA started asking questions:

- Who decided on the hours of work that Cheryl preformed?
- What was the risk involved for Cheryl? Was there a chance of a greater profit for Cheryl?
- Did the tasks performed by Cheryl integrate with the business?
- Who supplied all the tools for Cheryl to carry out her tasks? (e.g. phone, computer, printer and office supplies, etc.)

In this case, Dominique set the hours and the job duties that were expected of Cheryl. Dominique also provided all the necessary tools for Cheryl to complete the work required and there was no potential of profit for Cheryl if the business was more profitable.

Based on these factors, the CRA found that Cheryl was acting as an employee. Dominique was fined and had to remit the previous two years' worth of CPP and EI for Cheryl, which included both the employee's and the employer's portion of each. This was quite an expensive error, costing an unexpected bill of approximately $6,850.00 plus penalties and interest.

Always verify if you are categorizing the people who are working for you correctly.

Where to go to get the right information?

Most people will rely on others such as bookkeepers or accountants to advise on what is claimable and what is not. Some will contact Revenue Canada directly to get specific direction to their case. It is certainly a wonderful option to speak with someone at Revenue Canada to get direction, if you can endure the wait times.[38]

---

[38] Canadians calling CRA facing longer wait times, getting unreliable answers, CFIB audit finds (Jan 2020). https://www.cbc.ca/news/politics/tax-canada-revenue-call-centre-1.5416775?fbclid=IwAR3IyNKnRFGUiK57wmVrzQpU48bYZdF-

When anyone calls Revenue Canada for clarification or direction, it is to ensure they are indeed dealing with a situation correctly. Often, the information they are looking for is indeed correct, or at the very least helpful. However, have you been provided with incorrect information? A recent court case[39] in 2019 showed that even the information from Revenue Canada cannot be relied upon as correct! This person contacted Revenue Canada for direction and was provided advice over the phone in regard to their personal taxes, the information from Revenue Canada proved incorrect. To top it off, there is no recourse for the incorrect information and the caller was on the hook for their misfiled taxes.

There are several potential reasons for this. Firstly, there are often several variables that the CRA agent on the other end of the phone is not privy to or aware of which may change the advice provided. Secondly, even though the call centre has experienced and trained staff, the level of training doesn't always equip the staff to ask the right questions. A senior agent can be very helpful, but in a recent case reported on CBC news, the answers provided by a Revenue Canada agent are correct only 40% of the time!

This is another reason why having an accountant as a part of your team is important. As your supplier, they are often privy to your personal and business information. As tax experts, they will know which questions to ask when contacting Revenue Canada on your behalf. Yes, even accountants contact Revenue Canada for information, whether to clarify or verify information, to ask for a ruling on a complicated issue or to ensure the steps they are taking are indeed correct.

Gq42puzaD8g9I3qXfhk2FBbaKfw

[39] Canadians Calling CRA Facing Longer Wait Times, Getting Unreliable Answers, Cfib Audit Finds | CBC News, https://www.cbc.ca/news/politics/tax-canada-revenue-call-centre-1.5416775?fbclid=IwAR3IyNKnRFGUiK57wmVrzQpU48bYZdF-Gq42puzaD8g9I3qXfhk2FBbaKfw

I still encourage people to contact the CRA for clarification for many items, I just would be wary if you are applying the advice. Verify the information you have received by running it by a knowledgeable accountant.

Ways to Avoid an Audit

As frustrating and time consuming as it can be for a business owner to stay on top of regular filing of remittances, filing them on time helps avoid audits in three major ways:

1. It limits the huge bill at the end of the year by remitting on a regular basis (either monthly or quarterly), making it easier to stay on top of your tax, sales tax and payroll tax bills.

2. It forces a business to stay on top of the books, which in turn, improves the accuracy of reporting.

3. Helps you avoid being the obvious choice for an audit. If you do not file your remittances on time or pay them, it is like wearing a bright red shirt in the middle of a crowd of people all wearing white shirts.

The requirement to stay on top of all your income and expense tracking provides the opportunity to regularly check in with your cash flow and stay on top of your business requirements.

Please note: the above examples are just some of the more common areas audited. Be aware that the rules and tax laws change frequently or are applied differently depending on a variety of variables. Make sure you check with your accountant and/or bookkeeper to ensure you are indeed tracking your income and expenses correctly.

3.12 Fraudulent Scams & Alerts

"Learn about how to protect yourself from scams."
– Fraud.org/alerts[40]

Money scams are becoming so prevalent that you will more than likely suffer some amount of loss due to one type or another. In 2013, approximately 60% of businesses had experienced actual or attempted fraud. In 2016, 74% of businesses have experienced fraud or attempts of fraud. The majority of fraudsters are from outside the organization, however 5% of fraud cases still originated from an internal source. [41]

These statistics are based on the ones known, there are many more unreported cases. In the past year, I have personally dealt with four separate cases of attempted fraud and another three not in my purview but happened in the same organization. These fraud attempts are often emails attacking your computer systems or an email that essentially provides hackers access to sensitive staff communication in phone calls or text requests. Scams have become a huge issue for businesses today.

Below are some of the top types of payment fraud:

- Cheque payment methods (number one in payment fraud).
- Wire transfers (second in frequency and increasing, from 14% occurrences in 2013 to 46% in fraudulent occurrences in 2016).
- Business email scams (also on the rise).

---

[40] Read our latest Fraud Alert to learn about how to protect yourself from scams that are surfacing https://www.fraud.org/alerts

[41] Scary Things You Didn't Know About Payment Fraud Plooto Inc - https://www.plooto.com/blog/5-scary-things-about-payment-fraud/

Some tips for avoiding a fraud scam:

- Ensure two people either sign off or are part of the payment approval process.

- Do not process any email requests without verbal confirmation with the persons or company directly.

- Use an electronic funds transfer payment type (EFT or AFT, automated funds transfer, etc.). These have a number of security features available to protect both the receiver and sender.

- If you still use cheque payment options, make sure your bank statements include copies of the front and back cheques, although most banks will only forward a copy of a cheque's front. This option has a small fee, but it's worth it when you are able to identify fraud and save thousands of dollars.

- Get tech support to ensure your emails are secure and do not click on links or emails with potential scam notices. Have your tech person set up other security features on your computer and if you are not sure about an email, ask.

Nothing is foolproof, so research your payment options and put some policies in place to ensure more than one person is overseeing all payments coming in and going out.

Most Recent Scams

Some of the more recent phone scams are very concerning as the caller claims they are calling from Revenue Canada or the CRA. They threaten arrests or jail time due to a fictious amount owed for unpaid taxes[42]. The recipient of the call is then asked for personal information, such as a social insurance number, credit card number, a bank account or their date of birth to confirm their identity. Providing these types of information to the caller is detrimental and often the caller can become threatening or apply coercive language.

In some cases, the caller will direct the person to go to a location and purchase iTunes cards or go to some shady location to pay by Visa. One of my sons was told to go to a location to pay what he was owing and it was a restaurant in a rough part of the city. I am so glad he took the time to confirm with me as I filed his taxes. I was able to confirm there definitely was no amount owing.

I, too, have received these suspicious phone calls, including a more recent one from the "magistrate" who threatened me with jail time for fictitious amounts owing. I immediately hung up, reported the call and blocked the phone number.

The CRA will never threaten a taxpayer with arrest or jail. They will also not demand "immediate" payment and most certainly not request payment via e-transfer, prepaid credit cards, bitcoin or gift cards (iTunes and others). They will also not arrange a meeting in a public place to pay an amount owing.

Another scam, recently experienced by a colleague, involves a fictitious CRA demand letter threatening to put a lien on a person's home. The letter received looked authentic, including the last three digits of her client's social insurance number. This fake demand letter even included a slip to pay at the bank. It took my colleague a lot of research with the CRA directly to sort out. My colleague's client did not owe the CRA the amount stated in the letter. What identified the letter as false was the routing information or banking information to where the payment was to be deposited—it was NOT a CRA account! No one would have been the wiser if they didn't investigate. In reality, the CRA

---

[42] Canada Revenue Agency - https://www.canada.ca/en/revenue-agency/news/newsroom/alerts/alerts-2015/beware-new-telephone-scams.html

provides several payment options for taxpayers such as payment at a client's bank, by cheque, or through their online banking.

If you receive a phone call, an email, or a letter and are wondering if it is indeed legitimate, contacting your financial representative, your tax preparer, or accountant, or contact the CRA directly to verify any balances owed and to report the suspicious correspondence. I also strongly suggest that you do not call back the number provided by the caller or respond to the correspondence you received. Call the CRA directly at: 1-800-959-8281 for personal taxes and 1-800-959-5525 for businesses.

For more detail on how to recognize a scam go to this article on the CRA website: "Slam the scam – Protect yourself against fraud".[43] Remember, protect your identity, avoid providing your SIN number and other personal details.

Whether you are a business or not, fraud and scams are rampant. Protect yourself and be aware of what is going on. If you would like to know more about scams and some tips to protect yourself, here is a list of websites to visit for more information:

Federal Trade Commission:
https://www.consumer.ftc.gov/features/scam-alerts

In Canada:
http://www.rcmp-grc.gc.ca/scams-fraudes/index-eng.htm

Better Business Bureau:
https://www.bbb.org/

National Consumers League:
https://www.fraud.org/

---

[43] Canada Revenue Agency - https://www.canada.ca/en/revenue-agency/corporate/security/protect-yourself-against-fraud.html

Federal Bureau of Investigation Fraud & Schemes:
https://www.fbi.gov/scams-and-safety/common-fraud-schemes

"Slam the scam – Protect yourself against fraud"
https://www.canada.ca/en/revenue-agency/corporate/security/protect-yourself-against-fraud.html

4. TOOLS TO MANAGE YOUR CASH FLOW

What is measurable can be utilized to influence an outcome.

In the first two sections of this book, we talked about tips for **making money** and **saving money** in your business. Now we will look at tips on **managing your money** by providing evaluation.

I find that business owners want to know of what they should be aware and why. Monitoring, reviewing, and evaluating may seem like the same process, however, there are definite differences and tools to use at various stages, at various stages of the day-to-day, and at ongoing or periodic intervals.

Monitoring: This is the ongoing process of regularly collecting and analysing information at its source. This is a continuous, daily process which ensures the correctness of payments, the weekly and monthly reviewing of bank and credit card statements, and the quarterly review of financial statements. Monitoring is the day-to-day tasks that are touched on in the second and third sections of this book.

Evaluation: This is all about assessment—assessing if what you are doing is making the difference you intended or if you are meeting the goals you had set out for your company. Evaluation starts at a number of levels or is specific, such as focusing on an advertising campaign and deciding on whether it made a difference. This is usually done annually, at the end of a project, during a specific timeframe, or after a marketing campaign.

Review: When looking at the results of an evaluation, it's important to then make adjustments to your current plan: How are you going to change what you are currently doing to change the results? Perhaps the evaluation showed you are way off the goal you wanted to reach. Does that mean you should throw in the towel? Or should you stay on the current path as it is resulting in a potentially better option? The review stage asks HOW you are going to do something differently. Perhaps you need to make changes in planning, advertising, products and sales, decision-making, or process updates.

A review can happen at intermittent times in the monitoring processes or after annual evaluations. Perhaps you have had a performance evaluation of a staff person. The review after the perform-ance evaluation will determine the steps to take in helping the staff person reach a certain level. Perhaps you need to provide more training, a raise for the work successfully completed, etc.

At the very least, an annual review when your taxes are being done is integral to the long-term success of your business. The key for true success is to have intermittent review processes throughout the year.

Ideas do come up at difficult stages in your business. At these moments, stopping, evaluating where you are, and reviewing ideas may affect change and outcome. If you wait until year-end, it is usually too late to make adjustments that could help you avoid pre-ventable losses.

4.1 The Evaluation Process

Sometimes, moving forward can only happen when circumstances force you to move.

Where should you start in the evaluation process? Customers are your bread and butter, so start with your customers.

Customer Input

One of your most valuable tasks each week is to set aside an hour of your time to meet with one of your customers. Spring for the coffee, sit with an openness to receive their thoughts on how you can serve them better. This is where you do a lot of listening and your customers do the talking.

I would suggest preparing at least five key questions for your customers:

1. Tell me about your favourite service experience you had. (It does not need to be about your company.)

2. What is the most recent example of how we exceeded your expectations?

3. What is the most recent example of how we underperformed your expectations?

4. What challenges are you facing (in the area of product or service we provide)?

5. What is one thing our competition does that you wished we would do?

As each customer shares their thoughts and ideas, they are making you aware of potential areas where you could improve.

Perhaps your competition implemented something you didn't know about. Perhaps you will be enlightened as to something you never considered could add value. Your customer could also identify weak-nesses within your company that you couldn't see.

Remember, your toughest clients are willing to tell you what you do not want to hear, but their information—or solving their problem—could make you grow extremely fast. Guaranteed, for every complaint, there are at least four others with the same dissatisfaction but are not willing to speak up.

The value of your customers' feedback is crucial to your success as they can share ideas on how to increase the value you provide. They may:

- Provide recommendations for products which you may not offer, however, suit them much better.

- Suggest what you can do for your clients that differentiates you from the competition.

Other Resources

You've checked in with your customers, now it's time to also include other key people who may have new ideas for products/ services, ideas that may not even have crossed your mind, or ideas about a totally new market.

Consider some of the following resources:

- **Your staff**: They are key to your success. They are often your first line of customer service and your staff can tell you what your company is doing well or not doing well.

- **Outside sources, business groups**: These are great at informing you of business issues or new trends going on that you may be able to implement into your business.

- **Business periodicals**: Reading articles and news stories specific to your industry will keep you up to date on upcoming changes and developments. In this day and age, change occurs so frequently that staying on top of trends can better position your company with your customers.

- **Other business owners**: Local or industry-specific, all provide a different view on happenings in the economy or politics which can affect business. This is an important part of being successful.

- **Your suppliers**: They can let you in on the latest trends.

- **Local educational organizations**: These can provide professional development and offer training to your staff about new or upcoming trends. With these organizations, you can also find trustworthy resources for you and your staff.

- **Your competition:** Identify what your competition does well. Are you doing it better than them? Or can you?

- **Look Inward:** Identify how you are different from your competition. Are the strengths of your company something unique?

Competition drives ongoing education for you and your business, you may even unearth potential which you previously may not have seen yourself. Competition identifies key factors such as the state of the market, changes and trends, what works and what does not. Analyze what your competition is doing well that perhaps you lack.

SWOT Analysis

During this process, create a SWOT analysis (strengths, weaknesses, opportunities, threats) for your own business with all the information you gather from your customers, your staff and outside resources. Below is an example SWOT analysis with key areas listed under each to help identify your company's characteristics in each category.

	Strengths	**Weaknesses**
Internal	> Internal resources such as skilled knowledgeable staff. > A new, innovative product or service. > What your company does well. > Any other aspect of your business that adds value to your product or service.	> Lack of marketing expertise. > Undifferentiated products or services (i.e. in relation to your competitors). > Resource Limitations > Poor quality goods or services. > Unclear messaging. > Things your company lacks
	Opportunities	**Threats**
External	> Under served or under developed markets. > Mergers, joint ventures or strategic alliances. > Moving into new market segments that offer improved profits. > An emerging need for you products or services. > Few competitors.	> A new competitor in your home market. > Changing regulations. > A competitor has a new, innovative product or service. > Competitors have superior access to channels of distribution. > Changing customer attitudes toward your company.

You will be amazed at the insight the above points can provide you. Interestingly, the ideas do not need to cost much to implement or initiate dramatic actions; often it is the small changes that make a lasting and profitable difference.

4.2 Comparative Statements and What they Reveal

All strategies start with knowing what you need and when.

I stepped into working for one small company during a time of great turmoil—there were a lot of unknown factors—from staffing, to contracts, to funding coming to an end. There was a lot of work to do but one of the most valuable tasks I did for this company was create a comparison document from the actual financials of the previous five years.

Under each of the five years, I wrote comments that identified the differences from one year to another, such as:

- In 2016, there were record highs in the markets for the commodities they sold.

- I discovered that three years prior, the company's profits were $800,000 and sales were 3 million. This showed that profits were dropping each year since and that the sales were down 83%.

- In 2015, the markets dipped below normal levels, leaving less money to work with. However, expenses were tightened up which offset potential losses.

- Under each year, I listed the contracts that affected the income levels as well as why expenses were high for one year over another.

- One year, staffing levels increased 30% to cover training and employment of extra staff required under one specific contract. That contract was soon ending, so we had to decide how long to continue at the same staffing level based on the unknown of another contract taking its place.

- I was able to identify areas where we could save money and renegotiated our insurance and benefit contracts. This created a savings of $6,000 over the year prior.

- Are the debts increasing or decreasing over time?

- I identified changes and trends in the marketplace.

This information was such a valuable exercise as it identified trends and changes you couldn't gather just by looking at a current year's financials.

Example of a Five-Year Comparative Statement

Income Stmt	Year 5	Year 4	Year 3	Year 2	Year 1
Sales	280,585	270,663	256,707	199,707	190,585
Cost of Goods					
Purchases	97,389	90,673	72,648	58,389	27,389
Supplies	1,859	1,695	1,559	1,258	1,100
Frieght	329	256	190	29	29
Total Costs of Goods	99,577	92,625	74,397	59,676	28,518
Expenses					
Advertising	3,779	4,155	3,764	3,779	3,758
Acct. & Legal	450	2,098	171	475	450
Bank Charges	3,332	972	2,827	1,831	988
Office	2,840	1,640	1,905	1,234	1,089
Vehcle Exp	4,149	4,261	4,229	4,149	3,522
Meals & Ent	1,537	1,264	881	537	490
Rent	11,257	12,799	9,800	9,800	8,800
Travel	714	778	809	741	505
Utilities	2,296	2,131	2,041	2,296	889
Insurance	3,785	3,450	3,045	2,025	1,104
Wages & Salaries	145,283	133,879	132,287	111,013	110,183
Interest	3,332	2,972	2,827	3,332	5,827
Total Expenses	182,752	170,398	164,584	141,210	137,606
NET Income (loss)	- 1,744	7,640	17,726	- 1,179	24,461

Use your income statements and balance sheets for the five previous years and review changes over the years, notice the reasons for any unanticipated differences such as increases or decreases. Note when there were any significant changes such as a new manager or a recession.

It is also important to compare your business's performance to industry benchmarks and to your competitors' metrics. Are you in similar industry norms? Is it poor management? Has the company over-extended itself over the years?

It is the multi-year comparative statement that shows how a company is trending over time. You can see how a company's operations translate into financial results, whether in a positive direc-tion or a negative direction.

4.3 What is Your Breakeven Point?

"Expect the best. Prepare for the worst.
Capitalize on what comes." – Zig Ziglar

Breakeven point is: the point at which total cost and total revenue are equal; or to state that there is no net loss or gain, though opportunity costs have been paid and capital has received the risk-adjusted, expected return. In short, all costs that must be paid are paid, and there is neither profit nor loss.

Are you making a profit, or are you, at the very least, breaking even?

As a bookkeeper, I have had the task of telling an owner how dire their business circumstance was becoming. The company was at a point where the owner was unable to pay bills within three months and they needed to seriously close the doors. So, the owner brought in an accountant to review what could be done. All the accountant came up with was, "Yes, your expenses are higher than your revenues." Really? That's it? Not one suggestion, only a strong confirmation that the company was digging a bigger and bigger hole each month.

In this situation, the owner and I had plans in place to keep from getting to this point, however, there were three key events that needed to happen to stay afloat. Unfortunately, these events were out of our control—they were reliant upon sources that could not come to agreement. Therefore, we started the necessary steps to close the doors.

In this situation, the company had to choose bankruptcy, so the owners spoke with a bankruptcy company. A bankruptcy company comes in to dissolve a company and wrap up, selling off any assets and dealing with any potential creditors and legalities.

At the time the decision was made, I was confident that if the company dissolved when they did, everyone would be paid. I was sure that there would be enough assets and funds left behind for all to be paid at a rate of over 90% to 100% of total owed. This included the cost of the bankruptcy organization's services.

Once a company signs itself and its assets over to a bankruptcy organization, all control is lost. Not only did everyone who was owed money lose out, most only received 10% of what was owed, yet the bankruptcy organization increased their fee several times over!

This was the first experience I had with a company facing bankruptcy and the owners took the steps they did for the best outcome. Therefore, the decision to close the doors made sense; they were trying to protect their staff and their vendors by closing their doors at the best time. Despite the company's efforts to take time researching their bankruptcy options and make the best decisions possible, the company still ended up with a bad name.

Remember, bankruptcy companies are just like any business, they exist to make money. Once the assets are signed over, a business owner no longer has any control and the bankruptcy company may do as they wish. In this situation, they did.

This was a disturbing experience for me and the business owner. To make matters worse, the sales taxes owed—the GST and payroll taxes in this specific case—were also only paid at 10%! GST, like payroll taxes, are considered trust funds, funds that do not belong to the company but have been held back until they are reported and remitted. Therefore, the government has the right to come after the business owners and hold them personally liable for these funds.

In this case, knowing the breakeven point was key in making a tough decision for this company. I only wish I knew a little bit more as I would have done a few things differently once the decision to close was made.

How do you calculate your breakeven point? You will need to know three items: your fixed costs for the month, your variable costs, and cost per unit. The formula is the following:

Breakeven Formula

Fixed costs /(Cost of your product – minus cost variable costs for each product) = the number of units you need to sell to break even.

Example:
Fixed costs:

Rent	$2,000
Utilities & Phone	$800
Computer programs & office	$500
Wages	$1100
Total monthly fixed costs:	$4,400/mth

Let's say your average cost of your product is $20 per unit. The average cost to you to sell the product is $11 per unit.

Cost of the product
$20 – Variable costs $11 = $9 per unit is the profit per unit.

Fixed costs divided by profit per unit:
$4,400/$9 = 488.88 units need to be sold to break even each month.

Basically, 489 units need to be sold or $9,778.00 made in sales to break even.

If you are aware of your breakeven point, ask yourself the following: are your revenues below your breakeven point? Secondly, do you have enough money in the bank to pay your bills (your breakeven points) for three to six months? If you have three months or less, you may need to consider scaling down or closing shop. You should also consider your seasonal fluctuations. There are times when you may need to reduce to a skeleton crew but have extra staff during the busy seasons.

If you are exceeding your breakeven point, this is a great start. If you do not overspend in other areas and diligently watch the outflow of cash errors, you have increased your likelihood of success.

Planning to Breakeven

Cheryl is a good example of a businessperson who was clear on her breakeven point, even before starting up her business. Cheryl is an energetic young lady wanting to start up her own retail shop. She had worked in retail for several years so was very familiar with the expected sales going in and out of that type of business, the trends, the nuances and the glitches.

I popped into her shop in her second month after opening the doors and Cheryl was ecstatic to share her happy news. Prior to opening her shop, she anticipated that she would need to bring in $4,000 a month in sales just to cover her monthly. She was also not planning to take a wage for the first year, had money set aside to cover her personal needs and extra to run the store for several months.

Cheryl was so pleased with herself for ensuring she had that buffer. To her credit, she exceeded her expectations in the second month by making more than her stated $4,000 in sales. She was officially making a profit! However, Cheryl is smart—she put aside those excess funds towards her business emergency fund. Cheryl was very aware that the spring and summer months would be her busiest, so she was already planning for the months when sales are likely to dwindle. In this way, she would definitely make all of her business payments for the first year.

A good indicator that you are unable to meet your breakeven point is that your debt keeps climbing every month! That means you are using your credit to float your business.

Know your expected monthly expenses for your business, otherwise, how do you know if you are bringing in enough money to stay afloat? Or perhaps you are only covering costs, which is great, however, are you able to pay yourself a wage? Whether or not you are, the key question you, the financial institutions, and other third-party supporters need to know is, "Are you making money?"

4.4 Your Financials Tell A Story

"By focusing only on the profit & loss statement,
it is as if we are driving along, watching only the speedometer,
when in fact we were running out of gas."
– Michael Dell, founder and CEO, Dell Technologies

When a person is doing the books for a company, there are a lot of transactions inputted into the accounting system. There are lots of small items and some very large items, but all these transactions tell the inputter a lot of information. As a bookkeeper, I can see who is doing what and who is not doing anything. When you have a manager, there are specific expectations—training and monitoring staff, being the stand-in, go-to person when the owner or key decision maker is unavailable. Well, when one manager provides munchies and coffee at meetings for staff, and is putting expenses through for events, getting professional development for their staff, creating and running advertising and marketing campaigns, these are all good signs that the manager is doing their job. When a manager rarely has any expenses, does not splurge for company meetings (all with reimbursement options) and is not incurring any advertising expenses, these managers are not focusing on their jobs and likely not actively engaging in their roles.

When I look at a set of books that track a project that is run by different managers working in the same company, I can tell which managers are actively working and which ones are just coasting. There may be many reasons for this: perhaps the ones who are coasting have health or family issues, or perhaps they are not aware of all the things they can do. As an owner, your managers will do as they have been mentored or shown. It all starts at the top, with the owner. An owner's expectations and modeled behaviour are a guide for managers. When an owner has regular meetings to touch base, keep updated on where their staff are at with meeting their goals, this type of active ownership goes a long way in business.

When an owner is haphazard with handling cash from the cash register or openly takes out money during the day for whatever they need, this behavior is now taken as the standard for the staff to follow. What we model, we allow. Owners typically do not understand the standards they are setting until a staff member is caught stealing and they point to the owner, saying "Well, you do it."

A Perfect Partnership

Larry and Jim were partners in a manufacturing business which they ran together for many years. They started off as the technicians and since there wasn't anyone else in the area to provide their specialized service, they decided to work together. Most people would prefer to run their own business so they can do things their own way, however, both gentlemen enjoyed their family time and time away. Working together provided the opportunity to meet both their personal and business needs.

Now, most partnerships can be very good if there is a clear and well-written partnership agreement. Unfortunately, most partnerships I have worked with did not start out with a proper agreement drawn up by a lawyer and I have watched very profitable businesses end up badly for all involved.

Larry and Jim worked well together, and they took the appropriate steps to ensure everything was done right. They had a lawyer draw up an agreement, they agreed on the same accountants and would share profits equally, through dividends, each year. When I started working with Larry and Jim, they would take these well-written and very informative financials provided by their accountants and just throw them into a drawer in their desk. They did not even look at them!

Honestly, I understand why they were not worried. The bills were always paid, they were paid a decent wage and at year-end, they always paid out a portion of the profits in the form of dividends. They really had a business that was steady and going well so why would they even look at financials?

For accountants and bookkeepers, financials tell stories, stories which provide a lot of great information such as warnings of changes in trends, high debt equity ratios, the types of debts, and changes in income levels.

For Larry and Jim, the overall profitability was dropping each year, there were government-imposed changes to their industry, thereby reducing the needs for their services each year. If they evaluated what the financials were telling them, they may have been able to thwart the demise of their business by looking at other similar areas in which they could expand their business. Perhaps they could encompass a different market or look at ways of innovating their services.

I find it useful to place financials into a five-year comparison to identify trends. Are there positive trends, such as increases in sales and a need to hire more staff, or perhaps there are indications of negative trends? With Larry and Jim's business, a five-year comparison revealed a trend of slowly decreasing profits and dividends, due to implementation of stricter regulations in their industry. In turn, this affected the number of clients and the ability for their clients to pay.

Let's talk about your financial statements: What does your balance sheet tell you?

- **Assets** = What you own. (cash, bank accounts, assets, accounts receivable)
- **Liabilities** = What you owe. (Lines of credit, credit card balances, payroll & taxes, accounts payable.)

- **Equity** = What your company is worth, aka, the difference between what you own and what you owe.

The balance sheet is what the financial institutions, creditors, and mortgage brokers will need if you ever wish to get credit of some kind. An up-to-date balance sheet can tell you and your creditors a lot about your business.

On your balance sheet, they look at the health of your business. Basically, if the equity section of your balance sheet is continually growing, this shows you are a healthy company. Remember, the difference between having more assets than liabilities is your equity balance. If your company is worth more than what you owe on it, that is a positive place to reside!

Let's take a look at a simple balance sheet and items for which you need to keep an eye out:

Assets

Cash: Is this being reviewed each month? Are there receipts offsetting the cash utilized? What are your processes to track receipts? Are all of these cash accounts being reconciled each month or are there amounts missing each month? If there is an even amount missing amount (e.g. $20) then I would be concerned that there may be some pilfering going on. More than likely, people forget to return the receipt for which the cash was utilized.

Bank account: Is this in a positive balance? If the account is constantly in the line of credit or in overdraft, this results in expensive extra bank and interest charges each month.

Have you seen your monthly bank reconciliations? A reconciliation is a true picture of what amount of funds are left in the bank after all the deposits, cheques and any outstanding payments are accounted. Reconciliations will find duplications, errors, missing deposits or payments (outstanding items) or even potential fraud. Make sure you receive copies of all cheques issued: a copy of the front and back of all cheques.

Accounts Receivables: How much in receivables are you carrying? How many are three months or more overdue or delinquent? If you have a lot that are overdue, you will definitely have cash flow problems as your funds are tied up funding other people or their businesses. You got into business to make money, not carry other's debts. If you did go into business to carry another persons' debt, you must have opened a bank!

Prepaid expenses: Adjustments to these can be easily forgotten once the year rolls over. Make sure those prepayments are accounted for or only carrying the current year's prepaids.

Liabilities

Accounts payables: The current accounts payables are those that are due and payable within a short period of time (dependent upon the terms of payment). Do you have more in payables than you have available in the bank? This signifies a large cash flow problem. Carrying a large accounts payable balance is a note that you may be incurring late fees and interest on late bill payments. Perhaps this is an indication that cash flow management is not being regularly monitored.

Credit cards, lines of credit: These are often revolving credit which is handy for months where cash flow is slow. Problems arise when these liabilities keep growing and you end up living in a line of credit. Businesses living large through their revolving line of credit is way too common of a problem. Not only is this problematic on your cash flow in extra expenses for the credit, it affects your borrowing ability should you ever require more funding or a business loan of some type.

Sales taxes: Ensure all the credits against your taxes can be claimed. In particular, your GST charged on sales can be offset by the GST paid out on expenses. Many small GST amounts are often missed on smaller receipts. Don't miss out on claiming these credits.

Payroll taxes: Have they been remitted? If you have a large balance (more than the normal monthly amount), be concerned — you will incur penalties and interest for late remittances. This must be reported and paid monthly; know what the average amount is for one month so that you will know if it is more and act accordingly.

The third part of the balance sheet is the **equity portion**. When a company is making money, good sales and/or good profits increases the equity section of the balance sheet, showing a healthy company. The true growth rate is the top metric used to figure out the future value of a business. Equity growth rate is much more likely the true growth rate of the company in the long run.

The reality is that most small businesses turn around and reinvest the profits back into the company to keep it going on a regular basis. Effectively, this does not allow the equity to grow. When there is a need to constantly reinvest just to keep going, then the company is not as profitable as its potential. This state tells us several things: that there is an issue with either the amount of sales or the profit margin is too small. Perhaps a company should be reviewing these aspects of their business and engage a better plan.

Banks also look for the **ratio for your working capital**. In order to find out what that is, take all your current assets — which is the cash in the bank and accounts receivables—and subtract the things you are going to pay out within the year, like accounts payables.

Current assets - the current liabilities = **working capital**

What you want to aim for is a positive working capital number. Good companies have a ratio of 1 to 1, however, banks far prefer a ratio of 2 to 1 as this is a sign of a healthy company.

Start by asking yourself these questions:

- How much can you afford to risk?
- Do you know how much in receivables you can carry and still pay your bills?
- Should you carry receivables?
- How many months of payroll can you cover?
- What is your breakeven point?

Your balance sheet provides a snapshot of what you own (assets), what you owe (liabilities) and your income statement (profit & loss). It shows whether or not you are making money. Most business owners are familiar with a profit and loss or income statement. They know it tells them how their business is doing. This income statement is also what a budget or cash flow statement is built around.

An income statement reveals whether or not you are doing well. As much as this is a key financial document, it is only as good as your understanding and interpretation.

A positive balance on an income statement is the goal, but it is the line items that tell you a lot. In the individual line items, you see the types of costs being incurred. I bet every new business owner is always taken aback when they see the actual costs associated with specific line items.

Let's start looking at this line item: bank charges. This line usually includes credit card processing fees and any extra deposit fees. This is going up each year and becoming a huge line item cost, just for customers to enjoy a variety of payment options.

The costs of accepting credit cards is rising so much that our universities and colleges no longer accepting credit card transactions for tuition fees. These fees are now only accepted in cash, by cheque, or through direct payment. Smaller items like books can still be purchased with a credit card, just not tuition fees. Universities and Colleges have saved anywhere from a quarter of a million to over a million dollars in credit card processing fees![44]

Each line item provides details and information. See where your money is going, look at the detailed line items and you may surprise yourself.

A business owner that takes the time to fully review their financials will be surprised at potential money savings or perhaps identify potential concerns which need addressing. Financials can be a valuable tool to build your business. Take the time to understand them.

---

[44] More Universities won't accept credit cards for tuition – The Canadian press
https://www.ctvnews.ca/more-universities-won-t-accept-credit-cards-for-tuition-1.415977

4.5 Monitoring Versus Knowing What to Look For

"Handle the situation before it handles you" – Unknown

Who is watching your accounts receivables? Are they being monitored weekly? Monthly? Is someone following up on the ones that are still owed or outstanding?

Miscategorization errors: There are standard categories for expenses. However, often expenses are entered into the wrong categories or too many categories are created. Use general book-keeping guidelines for standard categorization and create as few new categories as possible. A large list of income and expense items can be confusing and is ultimately useless due to common miscategorization errors.

Again, this is where Reconciliations will catch a lot of these types of expenses. Another way to catch miscategorized items is to print out a detailed listing of the general ledger and have the owner go through the entries. This is a great exercise—an owner may not realize how much they are spending in certain categories. They may also catch items that should be listed under a different area or may find there are missing entries.

This is a great tool to practice with all your business owners on a quarterly basis.

Some owners may not be interested in looking into this, but some will take a very careful and detailed look at bank reconciliations. This type of owner pays attention to detail—he cares that his business is successful and will pay attention to the details of his business.

The role of a bookkeeper or accountant is to decipher what the financials are telling you and to identify where there are concerns. If a business owner is responsive to the information, they may change or adjust their plan or strategy based upon what the financials are saying.

Reconciliation: One of the fundamental aspects of bookkeeping is reconciling the books and bank statements every month. Nonetheless, there are businesses that do not do this and others where errors are made by not doing it properly. Again, this is a good reason for hiring an experienced bookkeeper.

Reconciliations of the bank and many other accounts are key to catching missing receipts, missing entries (due to information not being passed on to you, i.e. a cash bonus to an employee), and more importantly, reconciliation is the tool used to catch our own mistakes. Being able to locate missing information and send a detailed report of items you need from the business owner is integral to being a great bookkeeper.

Missing out on differences: Often, during the reconciliations process, there may be a small difference that they cannot seem to locate. In some cases, under a $1.00, I will just post the difference to bank charges. Spending an hour to locate $0.90 is not worth my time. Often, differences can include an amount slightly different from what was on the cheque and what was posted in the bank account. Yes, the bank does make errors. Sometimes they double-charge a fee, or transpose the numbers, or perhaps whoever wrote the cheque made the errors.

As much as it may be a small amount, it the reason reconciliations are done is to find errors, like the common ones listed, but also to locate missing items. Let's say you are out by $10.00. You may be tempted to just post to bank charges and move on. But by being thorough, you discover that a $1,000.00 deposit to the account was not posted and a $990.00 expense payment was also missing. These are huge differences and absolutely should be located. An amount of $1,000 and its missing sales taxes can be a costly mistake. Also, missing a large expense can also affect how much you can write off against the income.

Reporting all your income is more important to the government than reporting your expenses. Your income will dictate the sales taxes, your personal taxes, and that has the trickledown effect for other benefits available to you.

Reconciliations of bank accounts, credit cards, receivables, sales taxes, etc. in your accounting software is the key tool to verify the completeness and accuracy of your records. Once all your accounts have been reviewed and reconciled, you will have a complete and reflection of your financials. This is when your financials become a useful tool.

Financials tell stories. These stories will help you evaluate and adjust, or change direction for your company. The more complete and accurate your financials are, the more useful these tools will be for you.

4.6 Stop Winging it and start Planning

This is where clarity happens.

Have awareness on how each decision is made can affect your cash flow either positively or negatively. It is the constant monitoring and evaluation of key metrics which allow a business owner to adjust their plan to either keep on track or to take advantage of potential opportunities.

Most people are afraid of budgets or do not feel they need to take the time to maintain one. A budget is simply a pre-determined plan on how to spend your money. It helps you to stay on track and shows you where you are in relation to your financial goals. Non-profit boards, regional districts, corporations all work with budgets. This is a valuable tool to see if planned project expenses are on track or not, or if there is income left over to finish a stated plan or project.

It is easy to get bogged down by the daily demands of running your business and it is easy to forget the bigger picture. The simple task of keeping a budget will help you find areas where costs can be reduced, areas where potential for increases on your investments are missed and so much more. The biggest benefit of creating and reviewing your budget is that it provides improved clarity and focus for attaining your business goals. The biggest roadblock to success is failing to plan.

If you completed the steps in the prior chapter by creating a five-year comparative statement, you will now have a basis for creating a real budget based upon averages from prior years for insurance, wages, and other items.

Step 1 - Building a Budget

Using your Income Statement from the prior year. Take the previous year's actuals from your income statement and use this as your budget's template. Use it along with the following questions and action steps:

- What is your anticipated income for the year? Always go with the lower end of your anticipated income levels.

- List all of your expenses. From here, look at each line item and verify if there will be price increases. For example, expect an annual increase for insurance and/or benefit costs.

- What are your goals for the year? Do you have any large projects planned? Are projects on hold?

- Do you plan on hiring more staff? What are the staff's training needs?

- Are there any changes of which you are currently aware?

- Do you have a plan to replace equipment? When you buy a $15,000 piece of equipment, you do not put the full cost of the equipment onto your income statement. It sits on your balance sheet and a portion of its value is expensed each year as depreciation until there is no value to depreciate. The purpose of this is because there is an expected value on the life of an asset. If the value of an asset is less than a year, then the whole cost is expensed. Consider setting the depreciated amount aside into a savings to go towards replacing that piece of equipment in the future.

- Do you have an advertising campaign planned? Allocate what you feel you can afford or actual cost if known.

- Do you have funds set aside for unexpected expenses?

- Do you feel you can cut costs in a specific area?

Here is a budget example:

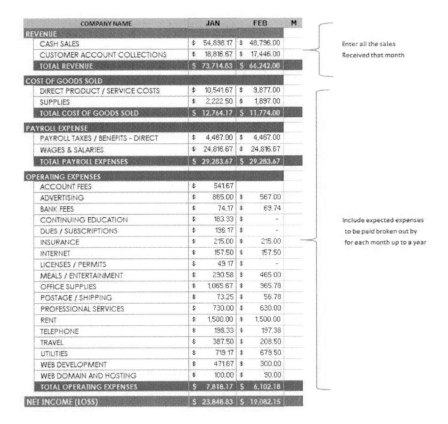

COMPANY NAME	JAN	FEB	M	
REVENUE				
CASH SALES	$ 54,838.17	$ 48,796.00		Enter all the sales
CUSTOMER ACCOUNT COLLECTIONS	$ 18,816.67	$ 17,446.00		Received that month
TOTAL REVENUE	$ 73,714.83	$ 66,242.00		
COST OF GOODS SOLD				
DIRECT PRODUCT / SERVICE COSTS	$ 10,541.67	$ 9,877.00		
SUPPLIES	$ 2,222.50	$ 1,897.00		
TOTAL COST OF GOODS SOLD	$ 12,764.17	$ 11,774.00		
PAYROLL EXPENSE				
PAYROLL TAXES / BENEFITS - DIRECT	$ 4,467.00	$ 4,467.00		
WAGES & SALARIES	$ 24,816.67	$ 24,816.67		
TOTAL PAYROLL EXPENSES	$ 29,283.67	$ 29,283.67		
OPERATING EXPENSES				
ACCOUNT FEES	$ 541.67			
ADVERTISING	$ 865.00	$ 567.00		Include expected expenses
BANK FEES	$ 74.17	$ 69.74		to be paid broken out by
CONTINUING EDUCATION	$ 183.33	$ -		for each month up to a year
DUES / SUBSCRIPTIONS	$ 136.17	$ -		
INSURANCE	$ 215.00	$ 215.00		
INTERNET	$ 157.50	$ 157.50		
LICENSES / PERMITS	$ 49.17	$ -		
MEALS / ENTERTAINMENT	$ 290.58	$ 465.00		
OFFICE SUPPLIES	$ 1,065.67	$ 965.78		
POSTAGE / SHIPPING	$ 73.25	$ 56.78		
PROFESSIONAL SERVICES	$ 730.00	$ 630.00		
RENT	$ 1,500.00	$ 1,500.00		
TELEPHONE	$ 198.33	$ 197.38		
TRAVEL	$ 387.50	$ 208.50		
UTILITIES	$ 719.17	$ 679.50		
WEB DEVELOPMENT	$ 471.67	$ 300.00		
WEB DOMAIN AND HOSTING	$ 100.00	$ 90.00		
TOTAL OPERATING EXPENSES	$ 7,818.17	$ 6,102.18		
NET INCOME (LOSS)	$ 23,848.83	$ 19,082.15		

Step 2 - Cash Flow Portion of your Budget

Add your monthly expected payments, loans, mortgage, your monthly payroll remittances, savings for paying your taxes at year end, savings for your savings. Add to your budget specific items affecting your Cash Flow. List the amounts that are paid out monthly or quarterly.

Example below:

Some of these items are found on the Balance Sheet not on the Income Statement and affects your available cash

NET INCOME (LOSS)	$	19,082.15	
TOTAL ADDITIONAL EXPENSES			
CASH DISBURSEMENTS TO OWNERS	$	5,416.67	Amounts paid out to Owners / mth
CHARITABLE CONTRIBUTIONS	$	60.00	Any Charitable contributions pd
INCOME TAX EXPENSE (remitted quarterly)	$	500.00	Amount paid or set aside to pay Income Taxes
PAYROLL TAXES / REMITTANCE	$	8,870.00	Payroll Remittance paid out to the government
EQUIPMENT LOAN PAYMENTS	$	460.00	Monthly loans paid out
SAVINGS PLAN (5% of gross income)	$	3,312.10	Money set aside for Business Savings
EQUIP REPLACEMENT SAVINGS	$	380.00	Money set aside for replacing equipment in the future
TOTAL ADDITIONAL EXPENSES	$	18,988.77	
Month Ending CASH POSITION (CASH ON HAND + CASH RECEIPTS – CASH PAYMENTS)	$	93.38	

Now that you have created a spending plan, you have a tool that gives you a really good idea about much extra cash is available each month to use. This excess or lack of cash will affect the decisions being presented to you each day.

Johnny, the mechanic I mentioned at the beginning of this book, had identified a need to add a mobile unit so he could help his clients whenever they were stuck. We put together his "Cash Flow Budget" for the year and these were the results:

JOHNNY's		
REVENUE		
CASH SALES	$	539,790.00
CUSTOMER ACCOUNT COLLECTIONS	$	189,750.00
TOTAL CASH RECEIPTS	**$**	**789,540.00**
COST OF GOODS SOLD		
DIRECT PRODUCT / SERVICE COSTS	$	128,500.00
SUPPLIES	$	25,670.00
TOTAL COST OF GOODS SOLD	**$**	**154,170.00**
PAYROLL EXPENSE		
PAYROLL TAXES / BENEFITS - DIRECT	$	53,604.00
SALARIES - DIRECT	$	297,800.00
TOTAL PAYROLL EXPENSES	**$**	**351,404.00**
OPERATING EXPENSES		
ACCOUNT FEES	$	6,500.00
ADVERTISING	$	9,380.00
BANK FEES	$	890.00
CONTINUING EDUCATION	$	2,200.00
DUES / SUBSCRIPTIONS	$	2,354.00
INSURANCE	$	2,580.00
INTERNET	$	1,890.00
LICENSES / PERMITS	$	590.00
MEALS / ENTERTAINMENT	$	3,487.00
OFFICE SUPPLIES	$	12,788.00
POSTAGE / SHIPPING	$	873.00
PROFESSIONAL SERVICES	$	8,760.00
RENT	$	18,000.00
TELEPHONE	$	2,380.00
TRAVEL	$	4,650.00
UTILITIES	$	8,630.00
WEB DEVELOPMENT	$	5,660.00
WEB DOMAIN AND HOSTING	$	1,200.00
TOTAL OPERATING EXPENSES	**$**	**92,818.00**
NET INCOME (LOSS)	**$**	**191,148.00**

NET INCOME (LOSS)	$	191,148.00
CASH DISBURSEMENTS TO OWNERS	$	50,000.00
CHARITABLE CONTRIBUTIONS	$	2,500.00
INCOME TAX EXPENSE (remitted quarterly)	$	13,500.00
PAYROLL TAXES / REMITTANCE	$	62,800.00
EQUIPMENT LOAN PAYMENTS	$	5,520.00
SAVINGS PLAN (5% of gross income)	$	39,477.00 *
EQUIP REPLACEMENT SAVINGS	$	4,560.00 *
TOTAL ADDITIONAL EXPENSES	**$**	**178,357.00**

YEAR-ENDING CASH POSITION **(CASH ON HAND + CASH RECEIPTS - CASH**	$	12,791.00

Step 3 – Evaluate how you can Improve, change, add to your Business:

With an actual cash flow budget, you now have a tool in which to make an educated decision as to whether or not yourself—or Johnny in this case—can indeed expand the business.

For Johnny, his Year-Ending Cash position of $12,791 is what is 100% available for expanding his business.

You may be asking, "What if he uses his savings of $39,477, as well as the equipment replacement savings of $4,560 towards his expansion? Well, let's review the purpose of these reserves:

Building a business savings is monies set aside each month for helping cover seasonal slowdowns or down times in your business. This allows you to continue maintaining your staffing levels, keep the bills paid, and have funds for unexpected expenses. These funds are crucial, especially if you carry a large accounts receivable as those funds are not readily available.

Equipment breakdowns occur, damages, and or unplanned increases in costs of supplies can really set a business back if there a percentage of gross income isn't set aside each month.

The equipment replacement savings is specifically set aside for replacing his current equipment and is based upon the life expectancy of said equipment. An example may be a forklift. Perhaps the purchase price for this piece of equipment is $15,00.00 with a life expectancy of 10 years. Therefore, each year, a portion of the purchase price is depreciated or expensed on the books, with the expectation that it will be 10 years before you anticipate the need for replacement. Putting funds aside each year allows you to have the available funds for purchasing another forklift after ten years.

Let's go back to Johnny's Cash-Flow Budget and use the $12,791.00 towards his expansion idea. With a projected income of $30,000 for the first year of operating this new mobile service, he would have approximately $42,791 to work with to incorporate his plan.

Johnny then went out and researched the estimated costs of a getting a lease for the new mobile truck, looked at the costs of the equipment required to outfit the truck, and costs of hiring a new staff person to operate it (included the costs of benefits and taxes to be paid). This all came to an initial requirement of approximately $83,180 in expenses for the first year.

Potential Idea to ADD to the Business

Loan for New Truck = 965 / mth	11,580.00
Equipment to outfit the truck	18,500.00
Hire new staff person to operate the Truck	45,000.00
Benefits & Taxes for Staff person	8,100.00
	83,180.00

Available Cash Year-Ending funds	12,791.00
PROJECTED INCOME for new SERVICE	30,000.00
at 2,500.00 / month for first year	
Shortfall of	**-40,389.00**

Johnny's business would take a ($40,389) hit. If Johnny used up his business savings and his equipment savings, it could potentially work, however, now the entire company is put at risk. The second year would see a potential of more income, and, yes, the equipment costs to outfit the truck would not be an expense in the second year, but there is the added equipment replacement costs which will need to be saved for and this is all on estimates on the income levels.

In this case, Johnny did not move ahead with his plan with his mobile unit. However, he did come up with a plan to partner with a person with a mobile truck! This was a great partnership as Johnny would pay commissions to the individual mobile service when they would bring new customers to Johnny's to service their vehicles. In return, Johnny sent his customers to this other company in return for a small commission. In the end, they decided not exchange commissions, but did refer clients to one another.

Johnny took this a step further and included this independent mobile truck operator in all his staff activities, including the giving of a Christmas bonus.

This was a great win-win solution

Now that you have your very own cash flow budget, you can use this to compare against the actual income and expenses, savings, and amounts paid out.

This provides a tool which, when used, will provide a story, a story which will tell you how well you are doing or if you need to change something. At the very least, it will identify where there may be differences and alert your attention to a specific area or areas where money might be being siphoning out of your business. It can provide the necessary warning bells to address issues before you take a huge loss at the end of the year. Or, perhaps you find out you are doing far better than you anticipated!

By doing this exercise regularly—whether it is monthly or quarterly, it provides a time frame in which you can still make adjustments to your business or help you address issues well before they get out of control. Avoid waiting until it is too late to adapt or make the necessary changes to improve the overall picture.

Budgets are a valuable tool for gauging how you are doing and how long you can maintain what you are currently doing.

4.7 Building a Bridge

Bookkeepers are your business bridge.

If a person wants a bridge built, who would be required? I am sure they would want engineers and specialty workers, all reputable and with experience in building a bridge. The structure and stability of the bridge is crucial if you want it to hold numerous heavy items such as vehicles of all shapes and sizes. You may wish it to be seismically able to withstand collapse in small earthquakes. For your business, bookkeepers are the bridge engineers.

The Redefined Locomotive

I, myself, have had experience with building a simple toy box in the shape of a locomotive for my son at Christmas. I had my heart set on building the toy box myself for my youngest son when he was just over a year old. I had done some small projects before and could use basic tools around the house, but building something with a frame was new. I believed it would be simple enough; I have sewed outfits following a pattern, so I thought this would be similar.

Before undertaking this project, I watched a few YouTube videos for tips, designed the locomotive myself, formulated a plan, and bought the materials I needed based on my measurements.

I was so excited about my project and proudly stated, "I got this!" Well, as I started putting the pieces together that I had cut out, one side did not fit. It just did not seem right. So, I switched the pieces and voila, it fit! A very different and unplanned shape of a locomotive toy box emerged. It fit, not because it was the right piece, but because I did not measure properly on one side or double check my measurements. Although it did the trick, my locomotive toy box did not turn out anything like the drawings I designed at the beginning of the project. To this day, I am still very proud of that toy box, unique shape and all!

We all possess different skills, and when we hire the right people for the job, they have the necessary skills, knowledge, and ability to complete the day-to-day tasks as well as the required reporting. Why struggle through on your own only to have costly mistakes?

Perhaps we should gauge the job by the size of the task. Building a toy box is a small task in comparison to building a bridge. As entrepreneurs starting out, many will choose to struggle through on their own until a catalyst occurs—they become too overwhelmed to take care of paperwork, pay the bills, chase down delinquent customers, etc. At what point should a business owner consider help? Perhaps only interim help is required or someone is needed to oversee and prepare the financials.

There are so many options. A bookkeeper or an accountant can help by ensuring key filings are up to date. This especially helpful for a new business, you may not have to pay your contracted bookkeeper the regular bookkeeping wages until you or your spouse needs more help. No matter who does the work, are you keeping up with all the tasks required?

Accountant vs Bookkeeper.

Bookkeepers build and maintain key bridges for a business. These bridges, if built properly with all the right structures in place, provides a stable foundation for a company to grow and potentially prosper.

There is a lot of different opinions and views on the roles that an accountant or bookkeeper plays in a business and often, they do the same work.

An Accountant is a person with specific tax expertise and can analyze and summarize financial data. Usually, they have a higher level of expertise as they attended post-secondary courses for a number of years and tend to offer more of an advisory role specifically with taxation advice & planning.

A **Bookkeeper** is someone responsible for the day-to-day recording of financial transactions, classifying with the focus on accurate record keeping. This process is instrumental in the ongoing financial upkeep of your business. Although there is no required formal education, the Institute of Professional Bookkeepers of Canada[45], is attempting to change that by instituting training and certification to promote a level of professional and ethical standards in the bookkeeping profession. Bookkeepers need to be sticklers for accuracy and knowledgeable about financial topics.

Bookkeeping	Accounting
Recording and categorizing financial transactions – as they occur	Preparing adjusting entries – usually at year end, and usually specific to the tax requirements
Posting income and expenses on a regular basis	Prepares financial statements as required by investors, banks, etc.
Sees the daily transactions – so they can be proactive in providing real time suggestions & advice	Only sees the books at year end – the advice provided is usually after the fact and is too late to save money in a situation that if caught earlier could have been avoided
Record Keeping - Keeps the records organized and lets you know what you may be missing	Financial analysis & forecasting - Involves summarizing, interpreting, and communicating those financial transactions. Many experience

[45] Institute of Professional Bookkeepers of Canada
https://www.ipbc.ca/default.aspx

Bookkeeping	Accounting
	bookkeepers can provide similar services)
Producing and sending invoices – stays on top of your receivables and tracks late or non-payments	Completing income tax returns – done annually, usually the only time business owners sees them
Completing payroll – including T4's, T4A's, other related slips and other remittances	Tax strategy and tax planning – Explaining the impact of financial decisions
Budgeting - Involves identifying, measuring, and recording financial transactions	Tracks a business's financial situation and conveys facts and opinions to the business's owners and executives, shareholders
Having a bookkeeper can ensure that government obligations such as GST, Payroll remittances, tax installments are made on time and you avoid fines and penalties.	Having a tax specialist work with the business owner, will ensure they have the best tax treatment and are able to identify available tax credits and can help advise on your business structure to best take advantage of any other potential tax benefits which may be available.
Having a professional book-keeper to work as an advisor alongside the business owner can help to alleviate potential cash shortages	Since a typical business owner sees their accountant once a year, duplicate cheques or fraudulent charge may have been missed
Hiring a bookkeeper to stay current can provide a savings of up to 50% on filing their taxes.	

Organized financial records which are regularly reconciled are produced by the bookkeeper. Together with a financial strategy and accurate tax filing by the accountant, their work will directly contribute to the success of a business.

Cameron McCool, in a *Bench* article, says, "Some business owners learn to manage their finances on their own, while others opt to hire a professional so that they can focus on the parts of their business that they really love. Whichever option you choose, investing —whether it be time or money—into your business financials will only help your business grow".[46]

Businesses need to find the right fit for their team. Regardless if you use both an accountant and a bookkeeper or just one of them, do you feel supported by who you choose?

Bookkeepers tend see your daily transactions, so they are aware of your spending habits. They would know if you go to Starbucks every day for that $6.00 cup of coffee or if invoices are not being paid in a certain time frame, etc.

The detailed daily goings-on in your business tell a story. If a bookkeeper is experienced, they will be able to read your story and let you know before the story takes a turn for the worst. They will also see the areas for potential improvement and can provide suggestions throughout the year as you need the information. Some are more proficient at this than others, and it does take time for a new bookkeeper to get the hang of your books and learn its unique story. Once they do, they may become an integral part of your team.

In an Audit, A Bookkeeper is Your Best Friend

In a previous chapter, we discussed the auditing process. As a bookkeeper, one of the key learning experiences I routinely go through each year is this process. By law, the annual auditing process is one many businesses for which I have worked must go through. These include government bodies, any business maintaining a trust account (lawyers and property managers),

---

[46] The Difference Between Bookkeepers and Accountants: Bench Accounting, https://bench.co/blog/bookkeeping/bookkeeping-vs-accounting/

non-profits, charities, and some industry-specific businesses. Some of these audits are third-party, others are internal.

For a number of years, I have routinely prepared three different companies for their annual audits. Every time, I learned a new process for avoiding issues from cropping up, a new change in the laws, something new to watch for, or ideas for best practices. I always found an audit informative and the fun part is showing the third-party accountants a new way of tracking. One of the biggest benefits of going through the audits is the constant need for keeping up with the ever-changing laws to which businesses must conform. Although I personally attend updates each year on changes to charity law, tax law, webinars on new software, new apps, and so much more, audits being done by specialists in their areas of expertise have taught me so much— I've learned tips for preparing and protecting my clients—the business owner—the best way possible.

Inevitably, I have had to track down a missing receipt or contract or have required more information. I can't stress enough that as a business owner, keep everything—receipts, invoices, bank statements, credit card statements, contracts, agreements, or anything that you may require to validate information. As stated previously, if you cannot produce the back up for a transaction you have claimed, the auditors may or may not disallow it as an expense, especially CRA (Canada Revenue Agency) auditors.

A good bookkeeper can save you thousands of dollars by discovering errors as they occur, hopefully in time to fix the problem! Accountants are helpful in identifying issues, but the annual visit with them may be too late for fixing an error, a double payment, or a fraudulent cheque. Timing can be everything.

I have also had the opportunity of working with brilliant accountants that can structure a business in a way that saves the business owner thousands of dollars! Accountants are indeed a must, especially if you have a limited company or corporate business structure. You will need their tax expertise to help navigate all the tedious tax laws affecting this type of business structure.

In general, I always suggest referring to an accountant especially in regard to business structure as the tax laws change annually. The benefits of each business structure can be crucial in your businesses tax planning.

I have also encountered the odd accountant or bookkeeper that felt adding up and/or including receipts is too time consuming, even simple things like including medical receipts! It amazes me that some would rather have the client pay more in taxes than save their client money. I cannot stress enough the importance of you, the owner, confirming that tasks are indeed completed. This check-in also ensures that nothing is missed.

A dear friend, Toby, ran a business for over six years and worked with the same accountant for managing his books and filing his taxes. Toby trusted his accountant to do what was expected and was under the impression that all was fine, until the day he received a phone call from the government wondering why he had not filed his taxes in over four years!

Toby was furious, not only had the taxes not been filed, he was behind in the regular sales tax filings! If the taxes were indeed filed, he would have received money back, instead, he lost some of his refunds to late filing penalties and was charged interest on the penalties.

Who is responsible for how or when your taxes are filed? Ultimately, you the business owner! You are responsible for your tax filing, you are responsible for your GST and sales tax returns, you are ultimately responsible and on the hook for your company's liabilities. Regardless of who you hired to take on these tasks, you are on the hook for late fees, charges and interest! Get the back-up proof that filings are completed. Also, either have online access to your government account to view the filings or at least ensure the correspondence from the government comes to you first so that you are alerted in case something was missed.

Now, in the accountant's defense, I found out after the fact that they were waiting on Toby to provide further information on specific details and were unable to file until the information was provided. Therefore, there was certainly more to this story than initially was admitted. This is just another example of a red flag that should have been caught earlier as there were definite indicators of a problem.

In another scenario, a business owner, named Alice, took her company's books to their accountant at year end for their annual tax filing. The accountant quickly identified that her bookkeeper, who was given signing authority on the business, was writing themselves large cheques which were clearly outside of the agreed upon contract. Having any bookkeeper with signing authority is one of the business practices which should be avoided at all costs.

Bottomline, "89% of business owners agreed that accountants are a smart investment"[47] whether this was based upon saving money, saving time, reducing stress, staying compliant or helping with planning ahead. It is all about knowing what to look for.

This is another good reason to have an accountant review the books at year end, as it is like a mini audit of your bookkeeper. Like a bookkeeper, an accountant is an important part of your team. However, a business owner with some financial training will always know what to look for and ask the right questions, reviews all the bank reconciliations, bank statements, and has a second signature on cheques if required. It is all about having the appropriate financial policies in place.

[47]Small Business owners agree, accountants are a smart investment. – Kim Harris https://blog.tsheets.com/2019/accountants-bookkeepers/accountants-are-small-business-superstars

Whether it is our staff, labourers, managers, accountants, or bookkeepers, all provide valuable and knowledgeable information, it is up to the business owner to make their expectations clear, take stock of what is going on and be aware of key indicators of a potential problem. Blind trust is not the most intelligent strategy for a business owner. In the story of Toby, an overall, better result would have resulted if only he had verified that the filing was complete. So "trust and confirm!"[48]

Xero recently did a key study determining that the success rate of businesses who work with a bookkeeper was much higher than those who do not. The study found that after five years in business, 85% of businesses who employed bookkeepers were still running. At the beginning of this book, I shared the statistic that only 50% of all small businesses were still in business after five years[49]. There is a marked difference when the right supports are in place.

Remember, errors do happen, things do get missed, and at times, these are out of your control. Perhaps the accountant or bookkeeper did not have all the information they required from you to file the necessary paperwork. Or perhaps they were not given the permission to proceed until it was too late to avoid late filings. Sometimes, facts and issues are not immediately identifiable until you can confirm. Remember, engage your curiosity if errors become repetitive.

---

[48] 2003-2019 ZD-CMS driven - © leadergrow.com Bob Whipple - https://www.leadergrow.com/articles/443-trust-but-verify Bob Whipple

[49] Make or Break? – from Xero
https://www.xero.com/content/dam/xero/pdf/Xero-Make-or-break-report.pdf or Technology and your accountant could be the difference between success and failure - https://www.xero.com/blog/2015/11/technology-and-your-accountant-could-be-the-difference-between-success-and-failure/

4.8 Create a Plan

*A plan for success is only as useful as the
actionable Items, listed and checked off.*

A plan is only as successful if you are fulfilling your business' core purpose. Why are you in business? How can you make a difference? Are you using your gift?

A Business Plan is a Roadmap

Your business plan should be simple, with clear, specific goals. Position yourself to take advantage of certain markets at different times of the year (for example, when things are on sale or employ bulk ordering). List the who, where, why, and how of your company and compare all your decisions to them.

Go back and review your goals on a regular basis. Take a look at and monitor where you are in relation to meeting your goals. This is a key step which many business owners skip. As Deborah Mitchell stated, "I take a look back at where I was a year ago and compare that to where I am now. That gives me a more accurate picture and reminds me that I am making progress, even if it's not as fast as I would like it to be."[50]

---

[50] 3 Signs That You Should Shut Down Your Business: Deborah Mitchell, CEO of Deborah Mitchell Media Associates https://www.entrepreneur.com/article/250267

This task need not be difficult, nor do you require a 20-page document. Start with writing down three key goals that you would like to achieve this year. Create a list in point form with your ideas or plan and how you plan to achieve your goals. Then, put deadline dates beside each point each task listed under each goal. Go back and regularly review where you are with each task. Are your timelines attainable? Can you delegate the tasks? This is the simplest, most effective way to tackle your list. I am sure you have heard of the saying, "if you fail to plan, then you are planning to fail."[51]

Here is an example of a person failing to plan who is paradoxically planning to fail: Let's say you decide to apply for what you consider to be your "dream job". You get a date for the interview, which you celebrate, but then you do not plan on how you are going to approach the interview. You likely feel that you will fail miserably in the interview and perhaps you will, so now you are just hoping that by some miracle you get the job. In other words, **if you do not plan, expect not to succeed.**

The whole purpose of this book is to provide awareness, awareness for the need for the right team, the right tools, and the ability to adequately monitor your cash flow so that you are able to evaluate your needs and review how best to meet your business needs. A simple plan is a good start on how best to achieve this goal.

If you want to really delve into a detailed plan or want more ideas, here are key components every business plan should cover:

1. **Cash flow planning.** What is the expected income or sales forecast for your business? Remember, everyone tends to overstate the potential income in this exercise. Achieve clarity on the expected expenses throughout the year so you can plan for increase need in products and the staffing levels required

---

[51] Quote by Benjamin Franklin

at particular times of the year (seasonal businesses) and planning for the downtimes of the year. Perhaps it is as simple as using the downtime in your business to innovate, develop, fix equipment, or get you or your staff specialized training.

2. **A marketing plan.** Market and customer research is important in clearly identifying your target market. Their traits, needs, and wants will dictate your marketing plan. Your marketing plan should detail your products, services, and how your target market can benefit from these products and services.

Although most marketing plans are developed at the beginning of a business, you should also review your marketing plan annually. Another aspect of your marketing plan is incorporating different marketing ideas at different times of the year so you can gauge the effectiveness of each approach. Erin Birch, a professional marketer and business coach I have known a long time has always impressed upon me: "When you learn how to market, you'll never go hungry."

Most business owners do not have a plan. Some have the same plan which they use every year because works. It could be as simple as the following, based upon the seasons:

February - Advertising blow out sale. Clear last year's stock and slash prices to bring people into the store. Mail out to key customers & employ radio advertising.

April - Advertising new spring stock, newest products or innovative products.

Summer – steady regular advertising and social media advertisements.

November – the big Christmas push. Mark down some items to draw people into the store. Mail out a catalogue.

You will notice there is different advertising and marketing used throughout the year. The benefit of trying different advertising outlets provides an opportunity for evaluating the effectiveness of each. This can inform if you choose to employ these same avenues the following year or change how you advertise.

> **Seek partnerships.** One often overlooked component of a business plan is including partnerships you can develop with other businesses. This may be as simple as partnering up with a business to share marketing expenses, sharing the costs of an event, or working to support one another's business in some way.

Another way to look at partnerships is creating a team of individuals that you trust. They could be experts in their field, other fellow business owners, or just someone that you can ask for ideas and the person will challenge you. Build your mastermind group.

When you are in a situation in which you are unable to see alternatives to a solution, it is usually because you are stuck within it. This is where a mastermind group of your own is key. They can provide tips on what worked for them, not necessarily what will work for you, but they can also provide insight or another way of looking at the same scenario. This often provides a way through that we could have not found on our own.

We all have well-meaning friends, all with their own opinion of what is right, but, honestly, another person will not truly understand or know what is right for you. However, a true friend will call you on your bad habits and support whatever decision you choose. The value in a true friends or mastermind group is that they will always bring another perspective to your thoughts without putting you down or chastising you. Who truly know what is the right path for another person? The role of this group is to provide options, ideas, or potential solutions, and at the very least, another perspective.

Ensure some key customers are a part of your mastermind group. As a mentor once told me, stop caring what everyone else thinks, but do listen to your customers, listen to the people whose needs you are actually meeting. This will help you decide whether or not to move forward on a new business idea or project. Your customers are the ones paying for what you, as a business owner, has to offer.

Schedule your action steps. Put your actions into a schedule. Ensure milestones are set. Do you have a timeline? Make sure your advertising for the summer campaign comes out before the summer, not in the fall.

This is just a simple plan of setting goals which you can review monthly. On my website, I provide free resources, one being a sample goal-setting sheet listing action items. I find when you actually take the time to write down your action plan and set a desired timeline to complete the task, there is far more motivation to actually follow through.

This is also a great guide to realize that if you are not following through, there is a reason your business may not be moving forward.

Follow through. The most important, and sometimes most challenging step is taking the time to evaluate how well an event or season went. If the event you planned was not profitable, check it off as something not to repeat or perhaps evaluate why it was not successful and change how it is done next time.

This is where learning opportunities and your mastermind group will be most helpful. their experience or their expertise can provide information to improve or ideas how to do something similar with a better outcome.

Taking the time to review your goals and how well your company did is crucial for long-term success. This review will change how you will operate your company in the future.

Business plans are not just for start-ups. Updating and reviewing your business plan ensures your business is meeting key bench-marks or goals you initially set out to achieve. Having points of measurement (goals) aids in providing a heads-up for upcoming changes in the market and so much more. Don't miss out on the benefits of having this evaluation piece as a key decision-making tool.

Using Performance Data

Have you considered reviewing your financial performance data against similar companies in similar markets? Doing so can inform whether you are above or below your industry's averages. Financial performance data can help you make key decisions.

For example, by reviewing how other companies with similar revenue approach advertising and marketing, you discover the average spending done on advertising and marketing adds up to 8% of their revenues[52]. If you are spending 4% of your revenues, you may want to consider boosting your budget in this area. Performance data identifies potential opportunities for making small changes. If you are interested in more statistics, go to the Government of Canada website: "Create a report — Financial Performance Data".[53]

---

[52] Marketing Budgets Vary by Industry, by Christine Moorman, T. Austin Finch senior professor of business administration at the Fuqua School of Business at Duke University and director of The CMO Survey.
https://deloitte.wsj.com/cmo/2017/01/24/who-has-the-biggest-marketing-budgets/

[53] Create a Report - Financial Performance Data, http://www.ic.gc.ca/app/sme-

Creating Supports

Think about the supports you require and provide them with clear direction about your expectations and needs.

1. What supports do you currently have in place for your business? Other income sources? Have you engaged other business owners for networking and camaraderie, family or friend support for childcare? List everything working for you now.

2. What or who do you need in place to help free up your time for working on your business? List all the things you need and write a list of services or supports that will facilitate those.

There are so many areas to consider when you create a plan. However, the clearer you are on your goals for each month, each quarter, each season or, at the very least, each year, only then can you break down a plan to achieve your goals.

Once you have written your goals, add a column beside each one with a note as to what worked and what did not. In the next column, put the updated date of your plan to attain your goal. Goals are just markers and each marker has information or outcomes that may change or alter your direction, most times, for the better. Then for optimum results, update your goal chart monthly. Do more of what is working and less of what does not.

A business will always have issues that require your attention: putting out fires, dealing with staff crises, or ordering for the next year. To increase your company's potential of success, try setting aside time to set goals and measure them regularly. **By creating a plan, you are working effectively *on* your business, not *in* your business.**

---

pme/bnchmrkngtl/rprt-flw.pub?execution=e1s1

CONCLUSION

Words don't teach, experiences and the sharing of our experiences are what help others discover a way through.

I would like to share a story shared by counsellor I have worked with, Adrian Juric. Adrian shared a story that was profound.

As Adrian was walking through the forest with a friend, the friend described themself as feeling "all twisted up". There was much turmoil in this person's life and they felt torn between allegiance to different people in their life. As Adrian and his friend proceeded down the path, Adrian saw a relatively straight stick with some nubs left on it where branches had fallen off. He asked his friend to pick up the stick and break it in two. This was a simple task as the stick did not present much resistance.

Later down the trail, Adrian spotted a stick, all twisted up, kind of gnarled-looking, so he asked his friend to pick up this second stick and break it. This stick would not break. Adrian then pointed to first the stick, which was easily broken. It had an easy life, there was limited turmoil. Looking at the second stick—the one all twisted up— this stick obviously had a difficult life. It had twisted while growing in order to reach for sunlight under difficult circumstances. As Adrian pointed out, "See how this twisted stick was resilient?"

This is why business owners who have struggled, perhaps nearing or suffering bankruptcy, can find a new way when they keep trying. They continually, and against odds, reach for the sunshine. Just like the strong, twisted stick. Their determination, and resulting resilience, empower them to keep on trying. This is what it means to be a business owner. Not everyone is cut out for the challenge, but those who are know that there will be challenges, learning opportunities, difficult times, yet have the courage to find their way through. Of course, there are also moments of great celebration!

Most business owners only need to read through Sections 2 and 3 of this book to learn the basic day-to-day financial management tools for running a business successfully. Section 4 of this book provides the tools for assessing "how you are doing" and for knowing when to change and or adapt to improve the likelihood of success.

Below is an illustration of the various aspects we covered throughout this book, the goal of which is increasing the likelihood of your business' success. If you take anything away from these pages, it is recognizing when to change, adapt, and look for other options.

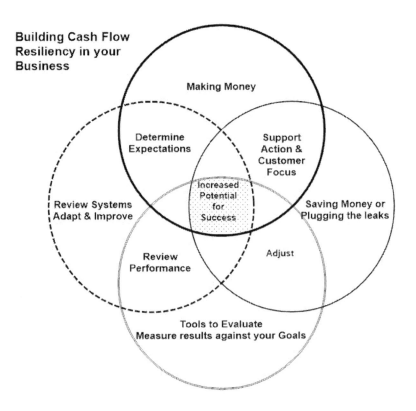

Building Cash Flow Resiliency in your Business

Making Money

Determine Expectations

Support Action & Customer Focus

Review Systems Adapt & Improve

Increased Potential for Success

Saving Money or Plugging the leaks

Review Performance

Adjust

Tools to Evaluate
Measure results against your Goals

In the diagram above, look at how each area is interrelated with others. This highlights the importance of how each area in your business needs attention to ensure all the key parts are working like a well-oiled machine. Focusing only on one area is not enough to ensure success for any business.

There are many bookkeepers or accountants which can provide the same information identified in this book and can provide value for you and your business. It is all about finding one that can understand your business and work well with you in identifying some of your stumbling blocks, help keep you compliant, and ultimately be a key part of your team so that your business can thrive.

As you take the steps to review your current systems and ensure that proper monitoring, evaluations, and review processes are in place, you may find that you need to implement a number of changes. Be discerning about how to implement and delegate—use your team, your staff, and ask them for ideas. Constantly evaluating and reviewing certain aspects of your business will transform your business.

If you come to the realization that your business has limited or stunted growth, sometimes the best step is knowing when to stop investing in your business and take the bold step of closing it down. You can always start up again with a different business—with a better vision, improved strategies, and clearer direction. In turn, this may help improve the profitability and chances for long-term success. Remember, some of the richest, most famous people in the world have failed in business numerous times before they found the right formula.

Not only do you want to be one of the 51% of small businesses still in business five years[54] from now, you also want to become

---

[54] 10 Things You Didn't Know About Canadian SMES
https://www.bdc.ca/en/articles-tools/business-strategy-planning/manage-business/pages/10-things-didnt-know-canadian-sme.aspx?intlnk=rightbox

one of the 85% of small business still active after seven years! Entrepreneurs are a valued commodity. We all need you. You are a driving force in our economy. You rock!

TERMINOLOGY

Accounts Receivables - Money owed to the firm, company, person for sales or services provided by the company.

Accumulated Depreciation - Pertains to an asset and the declining value of the asset over a predetermined timeframe. The amount depreciated should ideally be put aside

Liabilities - Are amounts owed to other suppliers, banks, loans, government agencies. A financial obligation. What you owe.

Assets - Are items of value either in cash or something that can be sold for cash including your accounts receivables as this is expected income. What you own.

Bad debt - Is an invoice owed to you that you do not expect to be paid or has been outstanding for over a year and considered to be uncollectible.

Bankruptcy -Is not having the funds to cover

Breakeven Point - The point at which total revenues equals total expenditures.

Collateral - Is something of value that can be used as security for an amount owed.

Company - Is an organization engaged in a business. The Business can be set up as a proprietorship, partnership, corporation or another form of enterprise.

Comparative Financial Statement - Presentation in which the current amounts and the corresponding amounts for previous periods or dates are shown side-by-side for easy comparison.

Current Asset - Something you have/own that one can reasonably be expected to be convert into cash, sell, or consume in operations within a year.

Current Liability – Obligations, money owed and expected to be paid within the year.

Current Ratio - Used as an indicator of a company's liquidity and ability to pay short-term debts. This is found by dividing Current Assets by Current Liabilities.

Entrepreneur - A brave soul with a desire to make a difference, armed with the knowledge and discernment to monetize their unique methods of providing a key product or service.

Expense - Something spent on a specific item or for a particular purpose.

Financial Statements - Presentation of financial data including Balance Sheet, Income Statement (or Profit and Loss statement) and Statements of Cash Flow, or any supporting statement that is intended to communicate an entity's financial position at a point in time and its results of operations for a period then ended.

Fiscal Year - A 12-month accounting period which companies and government use for financial reporting for tax purposes.

Fraud - Willful misrepresentation or deception intended to result in a financial or personal gain, inflicting damage on another person.

Income -Money received for service or products sold.

Income Statement - Summary of the revenues and expenses over a period of time.

Incorporation - Process by which a company is constituted as a legal business structure

Input Tax Credits - This is the amounts paid out on legitimate business expenses. These credits offset the GST/HST collected on invoices.

Insolvent / Insolvency - Inability to pay one's debts when due.

Integrative complexity - Basically, it states that a person whom can interpret and integrate multiple perspectives and possibilities, enabling them to come up with variety of contingencies. Being able to see the big picture down to the smallest details was s a common thought process among these business owners.

Invoice - Bill prepared by a seller of goods or services and submitted to the purchaser.

Loan - Transaction wherein an owner of property, called the lender allows another party, the borrower, to use the property.

Loss - Excess of expenses over revenues for a period or activity. Also, an amount of money lost by a business or organization.

Net Assets - Excess of the value of securities owned, cash, receivables, over the liabilities of the company.

Net Current Assets - Difference between current assets and current liabilities; another name for working capital.

Net Income - When total revenues exceed expenses, resulting in a gain for an Accounting period.

Net Loss - When expenses exceed revenues over a period of time.

Outstanding - Unpaid.

Owner's Equity - The investment in a business minus the owner draws or withdrawals from the business.

Profit - Positive difference that results from selling products and services for more than the cost of producing these goods and services.

Proprietorship - Business owned by an individual. Without the limited liability protection of a corporation or a limited liability company (LLC). Also known as sole proprietorship.

Revenues - Sales of products, merchandise, and services, and earnings from securities.

Risk - Measurable possibility of losing or not gaining value.

Sale - Any exchange of goods or services for money.

Tax Year -The period used to compute a taxpayer's taxable income. It is an annual period that is either a calendar year, FISCAL YEAR or fractional part of a year for which the return is made.

Trust Account - Funds being overseen by a trustee (i.e. Property manager, lawyer, etc.) which does not belong to the trustee, but to the prenominated beneficiary (owners of rentals, house sale funds, etc.)

Value - How much money something is worth.

Withholding Amount - An amount withheld or deducted from employee salaries by the employer and paid by the employer, for the employee, to the proper authority. These are considered trust funds as they belong to the government.

Working capital - Is a financial metric which represents operating liquidity available to a business, organization or other entity. Working capital is considered a part of operating capital. Working capital is a measure of a company's ability to meet short-term obligations. This is calculated as the current assets minus the current liabilities.

ABOUT THE AUTHOR

Rinette Lagace is a Certified Professional Bookkeeper with the IPBC (Institute of Professional Bookkeepers of Canada). She is also a Certified Non-Profit Accounting Professional.

She has over 25 years of experience in several business types, from non-profits to large corporations. In the field of bookkeeping, there is no substitute for experience. Bookkeeping processes are very specialized and can vary by sector. Therefore, a great book-keeper is one with experience in the industry, who can understand essential business operations, and can identify ways to simplify processes and eliminate waste.

Rinette is committed to professional development and attends annual educational updates and courses to stay on top of trends, new apps and, of course, the ever-changing laws affecting business and taxes. Her focus is on being a "solutions-based bookkeeper", always looking for ways to make it easier for a business owner to collect and track the necessary information required.

Bookkeepers must work with people at every level of an organization. They have time-defined tasks, and one who can commun-icate their needs effectively is an invaluable asset to a business. If a bookkeeper doesn't understand something, a strong one is willing to ask for clarification, sooner rather than later.

RESOURCES

For free resources, go to my website:
www.thecourageousentrepreneur.ca

    To download free templates:
        Payroll Tracking
        Cash Flow Budget

"The Courageous Entrepreneur Series" is a seven-week program covering the following aspects:

- Strategies to stay on top of your regular and intermittent bills and expenses
- How to avoid unnecessary charges
- Discovering frequently missed business expenses
- Knowing how to use and understand your financials as a tool in your business to plan for success
- How to use tools to measure your success
- Free templates
- Top apps for making your business easier to manage
- How to create a plan
- Valuable resources: where to find answers

Go to www.thecourageousentrepreneur.ca to sign up for my "The Courageous Entrepreneur Series."

Manufactured by Amazon.ca
Bolton, ON

11314000R00114